Rocky Road is not Just an Ice Cream

An Accumulation of Amusing Anecdotes

*Jo —
You are the sweetest, funniest gal I know!!*

By Bonnie Willemssen

Bonnie Willemssen

Copyright 2012 Bonnie Willemssen

All rights reserved.

Contents

Introduction..vii

Section 1: Nostalgia –
or why didn't I learn from the past?

Critters in the Closet...1

Pardon Me?..3

Do You Hear What I Hear?......................................6

Have I Got a Cliché For You....................................9

Section 2: Getting Older -
or why didn't someone tell me getting old is a pain in the behind?

The Joys Of Retirement..14

Rocky Road Is Not Just An Ice Cream..................17

Mi Casa Es Su Casa..20

Out With the Old...23

Expiration Dates...25

Cane And Able...27

A Rose By Any Other Name..................................30

Grumpy Old Woman...32

Section 3: Holidays -
or why didn't we just go out to eat?

Gobbly Gook..36

Let It Snow?..39

Missive On Christmas Letters................................42

Dear Mrs. Claus...45

Hippy, Hippy New Year..48
Like Sands through the Hourglass................................52
The Magic of Memories..54

Section 4: Love and Marriage -
or why didn't I get all that cool stuff when I got married?

What's In a Name?..58
Let Me Call You Sweetheart..60
Here Comes the Mother of the Bride............................63
To Have and To Hold...66
Trust Me..69
Till Death Do Us Part...72

Section 5: Tidbits -
or why don't these have a unifying theme?

When the Saints Come Marching In.............................76
Join the Club...78
First Class? Any Class? No Class!...................................81
Go With the Flow...84
Needless To Say...87
Go Team, Go!..92
Around The World in 80 Hours....................................95
It Was a Dark and Stormy Night...................................99
Sticks and Stones May Break Your Bones,
but Words Can Hurt Forever..101
Baubles and Bangles and Bling, Oh My!.....................104
Writer's Blockage...107

Acknowledgments...110

I give equal credit to my husband, Jim, and my daughter, Ann, who have endured being the subject of so many of my columns. Neither one has ever said I'm nuts, although I'm pretty sure they talk about me behind my back.

When I was in fifth grade, my teacher wrote on the top of my short story assignment "Very Creative". That was the moment I decided I was destined to write the "great American novel". But my ever practical father said "Absolutely not. You can never make any money writing books. You will be an elementary teacher so when your husband dies, you can substitute teach and have an income." I also must mention my mother, because where would we be if we couldn't blame our mothers for everything?

Introduction

I wrote these stories because they reflected my process through life. I'm now the grumpy old woman looking back on life through smudged glasses. I write with whimsicality and hyperbole so that no one takes me too seriously—including me. Since I can't go back and change anything, I try to find a way to remember it with a slightly different slant. Okay; some of it is pure fantasy. I mean, do you really want to know that the minute I enter a room I scope out the bathrooms first, then the food, then the seating possibilities, and then, only then, if there are any good-looking gents?

In the old days, before sags and wrinkles and prunes, I would have checked out the eligible men. Well, of course, that was many years ago—after all, as you will discover by reading these stories, I've been happily married for 40 years. Whoever said ageing is not for sissies was sure right. So, read on, and I hope you enjoy tripping down *Elder*berry Lane with me, skipping through the middle years as I discuss topics such as…umm, let's see…ahh, memory loss, and hip-hopping into maturity where so many delights await you—tinnitus, floaters in your eyes, bran flakes and *BEANO*, joint replacements, AARP (ALWAYS AGING REGARDLESS of PILLS), old people, care facilities, and don't forget love handles the size of canoes.

*Section 1: Nostalgia –
or why didn't I learn from the past?*

Critters in the Closet

My mother was part of the "dead animals on your body" generation. All fur coat wearers claimed their fur coats were for warmth, but we know they also represented class status. I was embarrassed when she paraded her furs at restaurants, on shopping outings, and in church.

For most of the long Wisconsin winters my mother wore her full mink coat or her mink stole, but sometimes if it wasn't all that cold, out from the cedar closet slithered *the fox boa*. If you're a lot younger than I am, you probably don't know about this strange accessory called a Kolinsky. A trapper kills an innocent fox and sews it into a slinky three-foot long fur scarf that wraps around a matron's neck like a collar. My mother's fox boa sported three tails. Why three tails, you ask? My guess is that some of the foxes that got caught in the traps probably ran off sans their tails and the hunters didn't want them to go to waste. At the other end of this oddity was a head with bead eyes and real teeth in a jaw that opened with a pressure clasp so it could bite its own tail.

Sometimes, expecting me to help her with things around the house, my mother would ask me to fetch or return the fox boa that lived in the closet. I would walk that long hallway, turn the handle on the door, open it a crack and slide my hand along the wall to find the light switch. Stretching in as far as I could reach without actually stepping into its lair, I'd quickly grab the fox around its middle as it lay over the perfumed hanger, keeping my hand far from his snapping jaws. Then I had to get the heck out of that closet before any of the other furs came to life.

I remember so well sitting in church next to my prayerful mother, the fox staring at me from her shoulder. Sometimes I could hear it whisper, "Bonnie, what are you doing?" I would try to keep my nose in my prayer book, fearful of looking in my mother's direction. Certain that she had raised me properly, Mother took all the credit for my good behavior in church, but the boa and I knew whom I feared the most.

Over time I became less afraid of going in the closet and discovered that there were many treasures that my mother had hidden on the upper shelves—old letters, old jewelry, old pictures. I guess she must have realized my apprehension toward the furs and thought that they were perfect guardians to her secrets. Did she not suspect that a middle school troublemaker such as I would eventually learn to overcome my fear of the closet and happily snoop when she was away from home? Eventually, the fox and the minks and I came to a truce.

As I got older, I dreamed of when I too would wear my very own fur. It was expected that every woman had one fur coat to her name. Mother was nothing if not a sterling example of how the upper middle-class woman should look. When I was 22, dear Mum, having lost hope of any gentleman asking for my hand and buying me a fur-lined gift, bought me an Alaskan seal coat. Several poor animals "bit the ice" to keep me warm. Of course, I proudly wore it for five years; the sleek lines and the soft fur made me feel grown up. Then, the enlightenment of the late '70s smacked me upside my head. People were becoming outraged at fur wearers. My husband (yes, someone did ask to marry me) and I watched programs about the brutality of baby seal hunting, the mink farm business, and how the poor beavers are mercilessly clubbed for their skins. Sad and embarrassed, I saw the error of my ways and hung the seal coat in *my* closet, where he languished for 25 years until I donated him to the church rummage sale. And that's the story of the critters in the closet. So, let's cherish chintz! Value velvet! Cheer for cotton! Rock on rayon!

Pardon Me?

"Excuse me." "So sorry." "My fault." "Love it." "It's perfect." "Don't change a thing." "I can't thank you enough." "You shouldn't have." We all say these words every day. We accept hostess gifts, smile broadly, state how it's just what we wanted, and then toss it in the re-gifting pile as soon as our company leaves. We are masters at disguising our voices to sound sincere; we have all perfected the false smile and we all know exactly how to make our faces show gratitude despite what's going on in our minds.

My friend Georgia told me a story the other day. She had loaned a CD of a great book to her neighbor. A month later the CD was returned with a lovely note saying how much the neighbor had enjoyed it. When my friend opened it, the CD was missing. Not wanting to embarrass her friend, Georgia said nothing, but a week later she was cleaning and found the missing CD on her own shelf. It had never been in the loaned case in the first place. The neighbor had never opened the case or listened to the book.

I'm sure those of you over 60 can remember the good old days when you received a gift and accepted it without question. If Mom gave you a pink fluffy robe, you squealed in delight, pronounced it the prettiest robe ever, and wore it for two years until it was time to get a new one.

Did you ever think of returning it? Exchanging it? Never. The gifts I got were permanent. If I wanted a blue robe, it was too late. Pink was my color for the duration. If I wanted a sled and got roller skates, that was my activity; if I wanted pop beads and got a ring, I wore the ring and kept my mouth shut. Parents, grandparents, aunts and uncles bought you what *they* thought you would like—probably what they would have liked when they were young—and you never questioned it.

A gift was a gift. It became part of your life. You wore the sweater with the cavorting reindeer on it, you played with the bride doll instead of the Lone Ranger and Tonto western set, and you had tea parties with the child-sized china instead of riding a new red bike.

For a while, during one of my "keep my hands busy" phases, I was making and selling felted purses as a retirement activity. A friend bought one of my creations for her daughter-in-law. She was so excited to send it to her for Christmas and couldn't wait to hear if her gift was enjoyed. Finally she received a thank you note from the daughter-in-law. *Dear Jane, thank you for the scarf you sent.* Scarf? Obviously her daughter-in-law never even took the purse out of the box. At least she sent a note, and though it lacked honesty, it had sincerity.

Why do we need to be polite? I think we would lose friends and family members very quickly if we didn't practice the art of politeness. I remember one holiday my husband saw an ad at the local jewelry store for a set of three tiny gold bands, each with a tiny diamond on it. They were to be worn together on your pinky finger.

On Christmas Eve, he handed me a jewelry box. I got butterflies in my stomach when I saw the size of the box and the name of the store. Inside I found a single gold pinky ring. I told him I loved it, but in my mind I wondered why he had only bought one of the set of three. A few gifts later, I was given another package to open. It was a different size box, but had the same jewelry logo on it. Oh boy, I had hit the mother lode—my husband had bought me two things from a *jewelry* store.

When I opened it, I was a bit confused, but tried to keep my face from showing it. It was a second gold band. "You wear them together," he said excitedly. Well, that was cute, and I liked it, but I thought, *why two different boxes?* Leave it to him to stretch out his gifts. I'm sure you can guess what I found in my stocking the next morning. My husband thought he was so clever. I laughed and relayed my gratitude. What else would I do?

Okay, now you're probably going to be suspicious of every word that comes out of my mouth, right? Does she really like my gift? Is she just being tactful? I bet when she said she was going to buy that very same pogo stick she was just being courteous. Did I hear her tell her neighbor that she was thrilled with the florescent orange bracelet her cousin sent from Utah? Was she just being considerate of someone's feelings?

Well, dear reader, I promise to love every gift you give me, so feel free to send them right away. And, I assure you, I will write a gracious and charming thank you note.

Do You Hear What I Hear?

Throughout my years in Catholic grade school the sisters and priests would tell us that we must seriously listen for the calling. If you didn't grow up speaking Catholic, allow me to enlighten you. *The calling* meant that God was calling you to the religious life. Whether they were priests, nuns, sisters, monks, or brothers, they all wore black from head to toe and seemed to float several inches above the ground. Priests were generally pastors, sisters taught or nursed, brothers were found at universities and caused the Pope great distress, nuns prayed 24/7 in cloistered sanctuaries, and monks didn't get to say Mass but enjoyed the perks of being able to drink wine any time they pleased.

During our formative years, the primary retreat topic was the *religious life* and whether we were ignoring that holy voice from the clouds. I spent many a summer day lying on my dad's lawn, looking at the sky and waiting for God to speak directly to me. I'm not sure what I would have done if that had actually happened, but odds are I would have run into my house to hide in the basement.

Our teachers told us that should we ever hear the calling, we should march straight to a convent or seminary and knock on the door. I worried that God would be so unhappy with me for not listening to Him that He would smite me right then and there, at the ripe old age of ten. I even considered entering the convent as a precautionary measure on the off chance that I was just too dense to tune into the Lord's radio waves.

There was never a saint's day that went by without a teacher telling us how lucky we would be if we were a martyr for the Church—a guaranteed first class catapult ride right past St. Pete and the Pearly Gates. Being a Bride of Christ (which is what a sister becomes after taking her final vows) meant being beamed straight to heaven, which is definitely a cooler form of transportation, and with far less of a rough landing than being flung by a celestial siege engine. To top it off, they receive golden wings and a complimentary halo upon arrival. Priests were the closest humans to God, so I guess they just appeared at the table of the Lord after they entered the great beyond. In case you're wondering, I did not enter the convent. Back then the decision had to be made by the time we were out of 8th grade.

It was in 1966 that a movie was released that almost convinced me that I belonged in a convent. It was called *The Trouble with Angels*. Hailey Mills, the young star of the movie, was my heroine. The plot revolved around the deviltry of two girls in a Catholic boarding school.

When the last day arrives, Hailey and her best friend are standing by the bus. The Mother Superior (Rosalind Russell) tells all those going home for the summer to board the bus, but Hailey doesn't step forward. Her best friend turns, shocked to see Hailey standing back with the sisters, most of whom had wanted to burn her at the stake for her misdemeanors just weeks before. I was as shocked as Hailey's friend.

Hellions such as Hailey and I could actually enter the convent? Had I ignored God's calling? Should I listen once again for the voice of God to enter my head so that He could elaborate His divine plans for me? What should I do? My mom and dad would fall into irreversible shock, possibly a catatonic state, if I announced I was entering the convent.

My friends would laugh for days, and what about my current heart throb? Fortunately, I was saved from further contemplation by the bell—literally—the phone rang. It was my best friend Mary inviting me to play tennis. I was out the door in two jerks of a lamb's tail and when I later recalled the angst about that important dilemma in my life, I suspected that maybe, just possibly, there was a slight chance I had let a silly movie influence me.

It's 45 years later, and I think I *should* have joined the convent. Someone cooks for the nuns, they never have to worry about the toilet seat being left up, there are built-in girlfriends to gossip with all day, worrying about what to wear is the farthest thing from an issue, and all that nice loose clothing means no girdle. Ever. 45 years ago I worried about what my parents would think; now I'm going to have to figure out a way to explain this to my husband.

Have I Got a Cliché For You

I would like to take you on a trip down memory lane. I feel so blessed that I've had so many opportunities to travel. I'm like a rolling stone that gathers no moss. Here's the long and short of it. My parents were two peas in a pod when it came to wanting me to experience the world. They tried to expand my horizons by leaving no stone unturned in new and exciting geographical experiences. Not one to look a gift horse in the mouth, I praise my lucky stars every day that I was privileged enough to be part of a traveling family.

Mother would burn the midnight oil planning our next adventure. All year she was neat as a pin, but once those travel books were strewn about the room we steered clear of her. She always said that too many cooks spoil the broth and we were wise to heed her wisdom. She could be as ugly as sin when she was riled up.

My dad, who possessed the wisdom of the ages, would beg her to cease and desist. It was to no avail. He could lecture her until the cows came home, but a pair of deaf ears were all that heard his pleas. He told me to be brave as a lion, ignore her tirades, and just muster my courage. Well, you know what they say, the spirit is willing, but the flesh is weak. I was armed to the teeth with trite remarks, but yet, I had to bite my tongue all the time. It was my worst nightmare. I thought that if I stayed in my room, absence would make the heart grow fonder. It didn't fool her for a second. She thought I was sick to my stomach, and when she discovered that I was just hiding till the coast was clear, she made me pay through the nose.

Rocky Road is Not Just an Ice Cream

When the day of our departure came, both Dad and I would be as meek as lambs, and off we would go, doing our best to keep our chins up. Mother would be in the forefront, fighting tooth and nail with anyone that dared to usurp or challenge her plans in any way. 'Course, it was no skin off my nose; I was happy as a clam just to be getting out of school.

Any port in a storm was good enough for me. Mother did have a good head on her shoulders and our trips always ended up being picture perfect. It goes without saying that she would be as vain as a peacock when it all went right. And did I mention pictures? She was stubborn as a mule when it came to taking pictures. It was no bed of roses traveling with a shutterbug. She was like a bull in a china shop when she wanted something, and she wanted pictures. *Lots* of them.

She wanted pictures of us in front of every known wonder of the world. Some of those pictures show me stiff as a board and my dad laughing his head off, and my mom, living proof that the hand is quicker than the eye, would snap away. I didn't want to bite the hand that feeds me, so I never complained.

I guess I'm just all talk and no action. Cross my heart and hope to die, I was quiet as a mouse or I would have been back to square one. My dad said I had an old head on young shoulders, but in reality I knew that Mother would make me pay for any insubordination by the sweat of my brow. I'm no dumb Dora; for all intents and purposes, reading people comes as easy to me as breathing. You know what they say—when the going gets tough, the tough get going. The long and short of it is that if I dared to put my two cents in, Mother would tell me the road to hell is paved with good intentions and I should just keep my own counsel.

To set the record straight, when we would get home, Mother worked her butt off on those pictures. She was definitely tough as nails, but she would just say it was all in a day's work and she liked being as busy as a bee. I didn't want to rock the boat, but I say that actions speak louder than words.

I was frequently finding myself between a rock and a hard place. I couldn't complain without getting my dad in trouble, too, and my ace in the hole was that misery loves company. I didn't want to push my luck. After all, blood is thicker than water. I've always been a cockeyed optimist with a heart of gold, and I figured as long as the right hand doesn't know what the left hand is doing, I could stay out of my mother's way. While the cat's away the mice will play.

Thank you for listening as I strolled down memory lane. It's been a real blast from the past for me. Actually, Mother's bark was worse than her bite and, although she never beat around the bush when laying down the law, she was my number one fan.

*Section 2: Getting Older -
or why didn't someone tell me getting old is a pain
in the behind?*

The Joys Of Retirement

I was so excited when we built our retirement home in Arizona because I was going to take advantage of all the classes offered in my new town. I was gaga over the course catalogue offering lessons in chess, jazz, guitar, Spanish, tennis, Shakespeare, astrology, writing, CPR, and tons more. It was outlined right there in the catalogue that you could move from beginner to intermediate to advanced.

Enticed by the idea that I could become *advanced* at something, I eagerly started with the introductory class in line dancing. So named, I guess, because they felt we needed to start at a level even lower than beginner. I knew I'd excel because my rhythm is pretty good, or so I thought until I tried to do the Electric Slide. My left foot forgot what it was supposed to do, and my right foot, apparently sympathetic to its partner, followed suit. After three classes—okay, it was actually only one class—I regretfully admitted that line dancing was perhaps not my forte, so I signed up for Painting 101.

With my 40 dollars' worth of supplies all neatly lined up by my lopsided easel, we were told that we would copy one of the five pictures at the front of the room. Rembrandt would have laughed hysterically at that prospect. What? I thought we'd start with two stick people and a couple smiley faces. I listened to the instructor inform the group that she was not going to go back to the beginning (meaning the class from the semester before) and that she was sure we would all catch up. Catch *up*? Hold on! I'm not a "catching up" kind of gal. I bolted for the door.

I chose my next endeavor—beading—because I thought it would be easy and I would have something to show my girlfriends at the end. The catalogue stated that we didn't have to bring beads as they would be provided for a nominal fee. Accepting the catalogue's word, I arrived with money in hand. The rest of the retirees, apparently aware of some important information that I wasn't privy to, had pre-emptively purchased beautiful beads of all colors, shapes and sizes.

The instructor's selection was not nearly as grand and varied. One hour into our two-hour class I knew beading was not for me. At the break I grabbed my completed necklace and half-finished bracelet and snuck out the back.

My next pursuit, Pilates, promised to strengthen my muscles and increase my overall fitness. I would be so dedicated, so toned, so buffed, so…wait a minute, did you know you have to get down on the *floor* for these exercises? When I finally managed to gracefully (read: earthshaking thud) lower myself to the mat without breaking any bones, the rest of the class were back on their feet. I only stayed 35 minutes, 25 of which were spent getting back up again.

Not discouraged in the least, I signed up for Indian Doll Making and actually completed the class. I still glow with the compliments I receive. Spurred by my success, I yearned to create a pottery bowl. I discovered there were lots of strict rules in the pottery room: sign in the second your feet cross the threshold, no loose clothing, don't use paints without permission, don't touch any of the molds or machines, don't sneeze, don't cough, don't breathe. I think the penalty for breaking any of the rules is being stuffed into a kiln and incinerated.

If we passed the introductory class, we could apply for membership to the Clay Studio. Pretty sure my pot is still sitting in the kiln. Do you think they're waiting for my application?

No, I didn't give up on my foray into finding something I could be competent at. There was chain making and silver smithing, diachronic glass fusing, and, ah, well, eventually I quit them all. I discovered that I'm very good at sitting, napping and watching TV. Why rock the boat? And besides, my favorite pastime requires no instructions—shopping.

Rocky Road Is Not Just An Ice Cream

Each year my husband Jim and I travel from Minnesota where we spend our summers to Arizona for the winter. One might think our adventure would be a pleasurable experience—sitting with one's spouse, spending time together, a chance to talk, no TV, no newspaper, no interruptions. No way! My husband is a point A to point B no-stops-in-the-middle kind of person, and I'm an oh-look-a-dinosaur-museum-let's-stop kind of person.

These marathon drives are so much fun. We make the 1,700-mile trip in one night because the love of my life doesn't want to miss too many football or basketball games. God forbid! When we get sick of talk radio, have exhausted all our books on tape, and can't find another thing to divert our attention, we have to converse. I happily carry my part of the conversation by reading all the billboards out loud. "Hey, cool, they can reverse vasectomies now. Those clever scientists." Jim's response is to turn up the radio.

We are a modern and enlightened couple. We share and share alike and that includes the driving. My husband always begins the first leg of our journey behind the wheel. Within 30 minutes we have to stop because our cat gets car sick, and I can't seem to get him to clean up after himself. Jim resumes driving, and I announce I'll take a brief nap so I'll be fresh for my turn. Three hours later I wake with a start.

"Oh," I say guiltily, "I bet you're getting tired."

"Not to worry," he replies, "your snoring keeps me wide awake." Once my eyes are open, nature calls. As I'm eyeing haystacks and telephone poles in a desperate search to find something large enough to hide my bare bottom, he manages to glide into a gas station. I rush inside only to discover I have to go to the counter for a key. As I wait in line, cross-legged, hoping that Bimbo Barbie will hurry up and pay for her cigarettes and Slurpee, I'm reminded of why I should do a better job of planning ahead.

When I return to our car, a super-sized diet cola in hand, I begin my shift behind the wheel. As I fasten my seatbelt, my true love fondly (read *annoyingly*) reminds me that I need to watch for the approaching semi, increase my speed gradually, lock in the cruise control, turn on the lights and remember not to go more than four miles over the posted limit. Finally, my eyes rolling back in my head from hearing the lecture yet again, we're off. A half an hour later we stop. The cat has thrown up. Behind the wheel, the daunting inevitability of three hours of ribbon highway stretching before me, I pray the caffeine in my cola will keep me awake. I struggle not to look at the dashboard clock as the minutes and the miles tick slowly by. When I can stand it no longer, my bladder bursting, then and only then do I sneak a peek. That can't be right! I've only been behind the wheel for 45 minutes!

Unwilling to let my husband know I already have to pee yet again, I divert my thoughts from my discomfort by singing along with the radio. I know my life partner is thrilled with my singing because he grabs the neck pillow and closes his eyes. I'm sure it must be so he can hear me better.

Sweet salvation finally comes into view. A Mobil Oil sign ahead, my agony nearly over, I pull into the station and hobble inside as quickly as my arthritic knees will allow. I search the ceiling for the restroom signs. *Please God, let there be a separate toilet for the women, let there be more than one stall and let there be super soft Charmin.* Even two out of three would be nice. On my way out, I stop to refill my soda. As I stroll through the door, blinking into the sunshine, I see our car heading slowly toward the interstate. My husband powers down the window and yells for me to dive in. He's definitely not a man that likes to dawdle at the roadside stops, but why would I hurry? I know I'll catch him in 30 minutes when the cat throws up.

Mi Casa Es Su Casa

"Of course," I said sweetly, grinding my back molars. I was once again agreeing to host people at our winter home in Arizona. My dream is to be the Hostess with the Mostess. I plan to cook meals, replace towels every second day, and have the newspaper laid out in the morning next to their coffee. After the day's fun is at an end and everyone is tucked in bed, I straighten and clean till midnight. By the third day I'm ready to collapse from exhaustion, yet I soldier on, organizing sightseeing trips, golf outings, and shopping excursions. I never forget my mother's Golden Rule: Thou Shalt Not Let Thy Guests Want For Anything.

I picture my company returning to the Midwest, relaying tales of my graciousness to everyone they meet. I can see myself lauded far and wide, a statue to honor me already in the planning.

I wonder if they thought I would put mints on each of their pillows at night? We actually have three bedrooms, but we quit telling people that. Once, during the mother of all invasions, we had two full-grown couples stay with us for seven nights—all in a row. As a person with obsessive compulsive disorder it nearly drove me insane. However, I never neglected to put mints on each of their pillows at night.

Perhaps a few of you might empathize with me if you've had visitors. For those who have escaped the perils of companyhood, let me explain. It always starts with the feeler. I can recognize it now in seconds, but when I was new to the visitor game, I didn't realize what was happening.

Picture this: I'm sitting on my patio, sipping a diet soda and reading. The phone rings. "Hello," I answer innocently. At the other end of the line is an acquaintance from back home. Chit chat follows.

And then she says, "We're thinking of taking a little trip to get out of the cold. What? Oh yes, it's three feet deep. Months of white stuff still to come. We just need to get away for a week. Huh? Well, we've been to Florida a million times. We want to go somewhere else this trip. Pardon? No, no, California's too crowded. Say, I remember you raving about Green Valley. We might just swing through for a night. What? Well, we'd love to. I promise it'll only be one night, maybe two. No more than three. "Can you recommend a motel we can go to for the rest of the week? We want to see the whole area while we're there, you know. What? Well, if you insist. We wouldn't want to put you out. You're sure a week isn't too long? Don't go to any bother for us. Just treat us like one of the family. What? Oh, you're such a kidder. I know you aren't going to make us wash the windows and clean the garage. Are you?"

That was the first year. The second year I wrote in my Christmas letter about what a busy schedule we had in our desert paradise and how we weren't sure we could squeeze in time for visitors. During year three I subtly hinted, in what I hoped was a friendly tone, that we needed to limit visitors. After a busy February in 2004, I announced that Casa Willemssen was closed for repair.

The following January 1st I emailed everyone extolling the virtues of our fine motels and included a list of phone numbers. The next year we put our heads together and came up with very creative lies about our unavailability. In 2007 we just left town when someone said it was their only week to be on vacation. "Sorry, we're going to be in Vegas," we'd blurt out. And then we'd quickly make a reservation for Vegas. No one came to visit the winter after that. Hmmm, was it something I said?

Last year we mentioned to friends in Minnesota and Wisconsin that it would be fun to see them if they happened to be in the area. This year I had to beg my best friend to fly down. So, okay, maybe a visitor or two now and then can be fun. But, you didn't hear me say it out loud.

If you plan to visit Arizona this winter let me know. We'd love to have you stay with us. "What, the second week in January? Oh, darn, we're planning to be on safari. Yes, we will be there the last week in March, but my sister-in-law's second cousin's brother's wife and her eight children said they would be visiting. *Next year?* Of course! We'd love to have you. Call first. I'm sure we can work it out."

Out With the Old

When are we officially old? In the newspaper it will say that the elderly driver of 65 was under the influence. Of what? Being elderly? Was she under the influence of sore knees, arthritic fingers or macular degeneration? Elderly! 65 is elderly? What happened to the *old* people of yesteryear? My mom and dad and their friends—they were *old*. Grandma and Grandpa were old. The scary lady down the street who yelled at us for stealing apples from her tree—she was old. She died at 101; now that's what I call old.

We try to hang labels on people to describe them: nincompoop; genius; simpleton; idiot; brainy; fool. The law uses *age* to determine when you can drive, when you can vote, and when you can drink, but where in those dusty old law books is the definitive number for *old* age? Middle age is up in the air, too. Is it 39, is it 42, is it 51? There should be a definition of elderly that includes a number, and I say that number should always be one year older than I currently am so that I never qualify.

Of course, there are times when I gladly embrace the term "senior citizen," especially when I'm shopping at Kohl's or Target or going to a movie. I proudly announce my seniorhood and cheerfully accept the ten or fifteen percent discount with flagrant delight. Have you had the senior coke at McDonalds? Since I'm "over the hill," I think I've earned the right to get it for 50 cents, although I kind of wish they would wait for me to ask for it rather than just assume I'm ordering it.

And what's with all the derogatory terms associated with old age? Grizzled, infirm, past one's prime, on the shelf, feeble. Some of them are downright rude, although I'm rather fond of the term "silver fox." That isn't to say that the compliment doesn't have its downside. It praises one feature and ridicules the other in the same breath, like when someone says you look good "for your age."

About 30 years ago my eye doctor told me I needed bifocals. "That can't be!" I exclaimed. He informed me that it happens to all middle-aged people. I was 34 at the time! The sting from that comment almost made me change doctors, but I realized he was just a young whippersnapper and his time would come.

It really would be nice to be *revered* for my age and wisdom, but I think I'd have to move to Japan for that.

And from what I've heard, if you're a man the name calling is even worse. They throw words at them like "old timer," "old coot," or "old codger." Who wants to be any of those things? And what in the world is a codger, anyway?

As a mature (as I prefer to call it) adult I'm very happy when the waiter asks our table of ladies, "What'll it be, girls?" I would have been incensed by that term 40 years ago, but now, on the other side of 60, I giggle along with the other "girls" at the table. And I've upgraded to a new insurance company that rewards me for my advanced years. It has great rates, but I grit my teeth every time I go to the clinic and have to announce its name—Senior Obsolete Medical Plus. The receptionist doesn't even look up from her desk to know I will need extra time with the doctor.

I did eventually accept that I was middle-aged, but I've been stretching it out for a looooooong time. Since elderly individuals develop salt and pepper hair, spicy personalities, and can sometimes be slower than molasses in January, I think the best term for those of us over 55 isn't *senior* citizen; it's *seasoned* citizen. This idea has been *marinating* in my mind for such a long time that I need a sandwich. Thank the powers that be that I still have most of my teeth.

Expiration Dates

Recently my husband and I have switched to organic products. Things like bananas and apples don't last as long as non-organic produce, but organic milk lasts longer. Why is that? I noticed my yogurt expired a week ago. It probably wasn't the best idea to eat it anyway, but, oh well. "Have Tums, will travel." With the price of food these days, especially organic products, I can't afford to throw things away. What's a little ptomaine poisoning? As luck would have it, I lived to tell the tale.

I have a box of warranties and instructions from the last 40 years; if only I still had the appliances that went with them. What happened to the lantern flashlight we bought in 1984? Where did the voice activated tape recorder disappear to? Oops, I found the operating instructions for the CD/AM-FM RADIO I sold at one of my rummage sales. I should have checked the box before I let those items leave the house.

What happened to the good old days when you bought a product and assumed it would last forever, or at least till you needed a new one? Computers are obsolete before you get them out of the box, cell phones are upgraded every year and our cable plan is more confusing than the schematics for a space shuttle. Just yesterday I was determined to figure out the functions for the 25 buttons on my new food processor. I conquered eight, and have resigned myself to be content to chop, grate, puree, blend, liquefy, masticate, eliminate and pontificate.

Rocky Road is Not Just an Ice Cream

Don't you think husbands should come with warranties? I wonder if there's an expiration date on the "I do's." Do you ever get to say, "Whoops, a lemon, I'd like my money back?" Not that I would ever say that about my husband. Heavens no, I have him whipped into shape now. It took me 40 years. I'm not trading him in, not without a guarantee of an even better-trained model. I've got him putting his dishes in the dishwasher (after prodding), lining his shoes up neatly in the closet (when reminded), making the bed (when asked), cooking once a month (if forced) and putting the toilet seat down (when he hears me scream). I have it made in the shade, right?

Well, I won't mention trying to get him to check if he needs milk before we get to the supermarket; that never sunk in. When it's cold I try to coerce him into taking a jacket or sweater; that falls on deaf ears. I beg him to throw his clothes into the hamper, but they always end up back on the shelf. I've given up getting him to work in the garden. And why, oh why, does he still use the dish towel to dry his plate when I have a designated plate-drying towel two feet away?

It was over 20 years ago that he said if he never had to work in the garden again he would vacuum every day for the rest of his life. I took him at his word—my mama didn't raise no fools! I guess I'll wait out the warranty on him and watch for signs that he's wearing out and needs an upgrade. I think he's surreptitiously watching me for the same reason. I bet he's wishing he'd bought the extended warranty when he had the chance 40 years ago.

Cane And Able

If only I were *able,* I wouldn't need my *cane.* Since last January I've been hobbling around with a cane. It's a wonderful, supportive device, and I'm grateful that it was invented. At first, too proud to accept defeat, I tried to go without one, but when sharp pain would catch me unaware, and I would wince and double over, it became apparent that something was needed to keep me upright because the alternative was falling on the ground and lying there like a turtle until someone righted me.

I tried a walking stick, but I looked silly walking to my table at the restaurant. I tried a leg brace, but it didn't fit under my pants leg, and putting it on the outside of my pants emphasized the enormous circumference of my thigh. When one weighs half a ton, it's not a good idea to make yourself look any larger than you already are.

So, as when I started wearing glasses, I shopped till I dropped to find canes in every color and style. After all, if it was going to be my constant companion, then it darn tootin' better match my outfit…or at least be cute. With my new metal friend at my side, I learned how to walk all over again. Believe it or not, there is a proper way to walk with a cane—and no, it's not how Dr. Gregory House does it.

Once I felt coordinated enough to venture out on my own, I didn't let my unreliable knee keep me from doing anything I set my mind to. Well, I couldn't join Zumba classes or join the tennis team, and that 5K was certainly out of the question, not to mention I couldn't—well, okay—

you know I wouldn't have done any of those things even without a cane, but it's nice to brandish my cane about and say things like, "Oh, gosh, I would love to help you move all those boxes out of your attic, but as you can see, I'm not *able*."

Before I got my very own handicap parking pass, I always carefully watched people who parked in those spaces. Did they look like they deserved that honor? Of course, I knew that some people needed it for asthma problems and other debilitating illnesses, but still, I didn't want anyone to take advantage. Now I have a handicap parking pass of my very own. And you know what? I still think about the legal issue; so I'm glad that my handicap is apparent to the other "judges" in the parking lots.

You may have gleaned from previous columns that I have a touch of OCD. Oh, okay, I have full-blown, total, unstoppable OCD. So, being fearful of the boogie man, shadows, basements, spiders, and being buried alive, I have carried various products that were supposed to make me feel safe and secure.

They've done no such thing, of course, but I bought each item in the hopes of feeling more in control. The pepper spray, the whistle, the air horn, my one-inch jack knife on my key chain, my cell phone—none have brought me the sense of security and safety that I get from carrying my cane. Any idiot who tries to steal my purse is going to get *caned*. Oh, boy, do I have to get a license to carry a lethal weapon now?

As wonderful as having a cane is, it's not without its problems. How do you open an umbrella with one hand? How do I carry my shopping bags to my car with only one hand? What do I do with the darn thing when I'm in a restaurant? It takes real management skills and sometimes creative thinking to stash my cane where no one will trip over it. Collapsible ones are a smart invention and are practically fool proof, thank God.

As frustrating as it can be sometimes to carry around a cane, it's certainly not without its perks. Teenagers, women, and gangsters spring to attention and open the door for me. I had a tattooed, scary-looking man wait for me to cross the street while he held the door open; I have had white-haired old ladies (even *older* than I) hurry ahead of me to grab the door and open it. I have had gentlemen from a bygone era contort themselves into pretzels to be polite and help me out.

I'm amazed at how my cane has brought out the best in human beings. I never would have guessed. My dad, the truest gentleman that ever existed, would have been very proud of his fellow countrymen and women. If you are old enough to remember the TV show *Paladin*, then you remember his motto was "Have gun, will travel." I am stealing that slogan and customizing it. "Have cane, will travel."

A Rose By Any Other Name

In the not too distant future, I'm sure my daughter will be checking me into a nursing home. I can see a typical day on Hallway Three. My memory will be failing, and I'll start to ramble on about my rich and colorful life and how it was accentuated by many grand affairs and several famous marriages.

Cary Grant pursued *me;* Grace Kelly was his broken-hearted attempt at happiness. Liz Taylor was crushed when Eddie threw her over for me. At the breakfast table I'll insist they call me Princess Anastasia—after all, everyone knows my unconventional adoption was because they're keeping my identity a secret from the Soviets. Aren't there Interpol agents watching me all the time? They're the men in the white suits I see every morning when I wake up, right?

By my midmorning pudding snack, I'll be telling the nurses they have me confused with someone else, because my name is actually Dorothy and I have recently returned from a wonderful trip to a place called Oz, where I married a tin man with a big red heart and played with a cute lion as monkeys flew over my head. That'll convince the staff to recheck my files and realize their mistake about my identity.

By the time I've had my nap and they wipe the drool from my chin, cooing at me and asking about the Emerald City, I'll demand an apology and state that my name is in fact Mrs. Rhett Butler and I want to get back to Tara as soon as they find my beautiful, green velvet gown. Fiddlesticks! Where is he anyway? I'm waiting to go horseback riding with him.

By lunch, while the rest of the residents are nodding off, I'll be shouting that my name is Amelia and they better get me back to my airplane if they know what's good for them. Don't they realize that people are searching for me and I have to get back to the United States or they'll think I'm lost?

During afternoon exercises, as they force me to walk around the garden, I'll tell them I'm Billy Jean King and I can beat any man on any tennis court. At supper, I'll be insisting that someone call the police to tell them I've been kidnapped by a bunch of lunatics, because I definitely know my name! Darn tootin'! I am Mrs. Dwight D. Eisenhower. Where are my secret service men?

As the day ends and I'm escorted to bed in my super-sized Depends, I'll smile sweetly at the handsome male nurse—I'm *forgetful,* not *blind*—and whisper that he can call me Mata Hari. When the sandman finally comes, I'll dream of my marriage to George Clooney. Does that make me Rosemary Clooney? Oh, wait, I remember, I'm the fourth wife of Mickey Rooney. Or am I Mrs. Andy Rooney?

Well, no matter. Tomorrow morning I'll be up bright and early to attend to my many commitments as Her Royal Highness, Queen Latifia. And by the way, my daughter is visiting next week, so please be respectful of her privacy and don't ask for autographs. Although, sometimes she brings her latest bestsellers along and she'll sign them for you if you fork over $29.99.

Tell the stately bellman to *please* take my bags up to the VIP Suite and inform my maid that I require my clothes to be pressed and waiting. I will need to look spectacular for my grand entrance at the ball. I hear the prince is looking for a bride. I'm planning to borrow some glass slippers from my dear friend Cinderella.

Grumpy Old Woman

It occurred to me that I'm becoming a crotchety old lady. I go into a clothing store and the blasting music assaults my ears. I try to ignore it while I go about choosing something to try on. I enter the dressing room and get angry that I have to listen to those screeching sounds—oh wait—that's the noise *I'm* making trying to pull the size-18 jeans over my size-20 rear end. There's just too much weeping and gnashing of teeth in the dressing room…well, I guess that's just me when I look in the three-way mirror.

After the distress of discovering that all clothing is apparently preshrunk, I like to follow up with a relaxing and delightful lunch. I rehearse what I'm going to order while I'm still in the car; that way I'll be prepared and not be tempted to overindulge.

My girlfriend is 20 minutes late, the waiter has not returned with my second iced tea, and the young couple behind me has a baby wailing at the top of its lungs. The man at the booth to my right is talking loudly on his cell about some business deal while he shovels meatloaf in his mouth. My friend rushes in, excuses at the ready, and the waiter finally shows up again.

She orders her salad with dressing on the *side* so she can get a teeny, tiny, miniscule drop on her fork before spearing the bare lettuce. If lettuce was meant to be bare, I think God would have made it a more appealing color.

I'm at the end of my rope; it's either turn around and smack the parents of the child or try to tune them out and avoid arrest. I order a triple cheeseburger with bacon and mushrooms, onion rings for a side, and oh, what the heck, throw in some french fries. Of course, after the waiter sees how restrained I am with my lunch choices, he's Johnny-on-the-spot when it comes to the dessert tray. I remember the nuns in grade school talking about the temptations of Satan, but I order the carrot cake anyway 'cause I know I need my veggies.

The grocery store is my next adventure. I weave in and out and around the myriad of grocery carts commandeered by people oblivious to the fact that other people shop in the store and *might* need to get down the aisle. Apparently they feel it's necessary to park their conveyance smack in the middle and keep a hand on it while they stand perfectly still and read the tiny words on the side of every box like they're studying for a midterm exam.

Of course, my favorite person is the one that plucks one item off the shelf, puts it back, grabs another, puts it back, reaches on tiptoe to pull another and puts it back. I've learned that the best approach to this issue is to ever so carefully move their cart because I know if I actually speak words aloud I could be thrown out for screaming profanities, and then I'd have to find another grocery store to shop in and, well, I'm running out of grocery stores.

Sometimes, if my gentle, subtle nudging of their buggy barricade doesn't work, I just give it a big shove and keep on going, ignoring the indignant protests of Mr. or Mrs. No Clue. And don't you just love the guy or gal with the overflowing grocery cart standing right in front of you in the "10 items or less" line?

"Excuse me? Did you notice the sign up there?" If only I had photos of all the shocked expressions. "Oh, my, I didn't see the sign." "What, when did they put that sign up?" Or here is the best, "Sorry, I'm in a hurry and this line was the shortest." Like the rest of us have nothing to do for the

Rocky Road is Not Just an Ice Cream

rest of the day? Well, I don't, but that's not the point. And what about the clerk in Macy's that talks the person in front of you into opening a charge account right then and there while you are supposed to patiently wait. Well, I'm not the "patiently wait" type of person. I wouldn't be a *grumpy old woman* if that were the case, right?

On my way home, I get behind a blind, deaf man—okay, it could have been a woman just as easily—with an excellent memory, as demonstrated by the fact that he/she is driving 20 miles an hour, the same speed his/her horse and buggy traveled back when he/she were young whippersnappers. And just having to be so politically correct in that last sentence makes me want to spit tacks at someone.

And isn't it a shame that they forgot to put turn signals on some cars? And since *when* is it legal to cut across three lanes of traffic to make a left turn and where is a patrol car when you need one… and did anyone in uniform see the idiot who just passed me going 65 in the 35 zone?

I finally get home. My husband apparently didn't notice the note I left taped to his TV remote control that asked him to start peeling the potatoes and browning the meat. Strange, the TV is on. What could have happened to that note? Having been married for 40 years, I ask him *sweetly* why he didn't do what I asked and what was he doing instead and how come he can't ever follow a simple direction and can't he read and when did he ever help around the house and how did we ever make it this long?

As I pause for a breath, he turns from the TV, looks surprised to see me, smiles and asks me when I got back and do I need help bringing in the groceries. He had no clue I was railing at him, engrossed in the seventh rerun of *Cheers* as he was, and I had to leave the room because you would be surprised how lethal a weapon the remote control can be when aimed directly at the head of the grumpy old *man* in your life.

*Section 3: Holidays -
or why didn't we just go out to eat?*

Gobbly Gook

Thanksgiving seems like such a family centered holiday, doesn't it? We're told that the Pilgrims, hampered by the lack of microwave ovens, happily welcomed the Indians and their offering of corn on the cob with fat-free spray butter. However, I'm sure that Mrs. Pilgrim turned to Mrs. Plymouth Rock and complained mightily about the extra dishes she was going to have to wash, and just *where* in the world was she going to find another card table and chairs at such a late hour?

In the good old days, before my daughter moved all the way across the country for a job, we used to have nice, homey, family dinners. In attendence were my husband, my daughter, my mom and dad, my aunt, my father-in-law and lots of extended family. But people started to die on us, thus leaving empty spaces at my Thanksgiving table.

We had our dinner tradition until three years ago when my daughter met "the one" and he whisked her off to London for Thanksgiving, where they don't even celebrate it. We told her we were thrilled that she would have this wonderful travel experience. What else could we say? So, off into the great blue yonder she flew with nary a thought for her poor parental units sitting tearfully at home.

Well, that's what we let her *think* anyway. What really happened was I looked at my own Mr. Pilgrim and said, "We're outta here!" Moments later we were in the car, headed for Arizona. We packed so quickly we had to buy underwear along the route. For the first time in 30 years I didn't have to pre-plan, dust, grocery shop, cook or clean up.

After dinner I didn't sit on the couch wishing I had bought my slacks a size larger, and there was no making small talk with the relatives while barely keeping my eyes open. We were foot loose and fancy free. We could eat at any restaurant we wanted, get up, pay the bill, and leave, though I did give the wait staff a sympathetic parting glance when we left.

That night we got an e-mail from our daughter in London. Poor dear, she was feeling bad about missing our traditional dinner, lamenting particularly about not having turkey leftovers for the next day. I e-mailed back saying how sorry we were not to be spending Thanksgiving with her, too. I told her I wished she could have been there for the splendid banquet we enjoyed and informed her I tried some different recipes, all without letting her know that I had hung up my chef's hat. I told her we hoped she could still enjoy her trip despite the fact that we were *all alone*. I'm pretty sure I kept the ironic tone out of my voice.

That was three years ago. Two years ago, if I remember correctly, Jim watched football all day, I read a book and we had crock pot lasagna for dinner. Actually, it was a wonderful Thanksgiving Day. I sat in the soothing bubbles of the hot tub and reminisced about Thanksgivings past. Nostalgia has its place, but remembering all the effort involved in creating those memories made me want to drown my sorrows either in the hot tub or a bottle of red wine. Wine goes better with lasagna.

Last year, Jim had the brilliant idea to have friends over for a *potluck* Thanksgiving. I agreed, but worried about whether they still sold butterball turkeys. Could I remember how to make green beans almandine? Was it in me to buy a pumpkin pie instead of making it from scratch? Ha, I'm just kidding on that one. If God wanted me to make pie from scratch, He never would have invented Perkins.

Where was I? Oh yes—agreeing to yet again be slave for a day. Problem was I didn't take into account that the women who brought food would want to be in the kitchen with me while I tended to my turkey. I don't do crowded rooms, I don't handle distractions while I'm trying to remember if I put the salt in the gravy or not, and I certainly don't like people wanting to help me in *my* kitchen. I tried to figure out a way to rope off my kitchen without being too obvious, but I failed. Who's the idiot that designed kitchens to have open entrances, anyway?

So, here we are, year four on our own. Our daughter is off again on some exotic vacation with her fiancé, while we are forgotten like yesterday's news. The best part is she still doesn't have a clue I'm secretly and blissfully enjoying my retirement from Thanksgiving kitchen duty.

So thanks, Pilgrims and Indians, for initiating the tradition of killing and cooking turkeys, harvesting carrots, beans and potato chips, and especially for spilling brown sugar on those yams. Luckily, women no longer get up at dawn and cook for 15 hours on Thanksgiving Day. Oh no, hunting and gathering has given way to shouting and high-fiving in front of a football game. *Ding dong*. Oh, sorry, I have to go, it's Domino's with our new Thanksgiving tradition—pizza.

Let It Snow?

What is it with snow? It tries so hard to be fresh and clean and bright. It may have millions of winter enthusiasts enchanted by its beauty and pristine charm, but I say go be bright somewhere else and leave me alone.

When I was little, I would go sledding with my dad. He would dutifully ride down on the toboggan with me, pull it back up the hill and off we'd go again. I begged to go alone. *Please, Daddy, just one time?* Foolishly relenting (you should never listen to your kid), he let me take that last run on my own. A toboggan with an eight-year-old on it that didn't know how to steer and had her eyes closed right from the top is not the best combination. I was saved from a concussion by a dad at the bottom of the hill, who grabbed me before I hit the pine tree.

I've always questioned people's infatuation with snow, but when you grow up in Wisconsin you don't get an option. In middle school I decided to give ice skating a try. My mother would drop me off at the rink and promise to get me in two hours. *Two hours?* I surmise now that my mom was probably sneaking in some shopping, or driving home as fast as the icy roads allowed with hopes that she could put up her feet, sip tea and read a magazine before coming back to get me.

Meanwhile, back at the rink I would lumber into the warming house, lace up my skates, slip on the blade guards and gingerly tiptoe down the scarred wooden ramp. From there I would take off the guards and glide onto the ice. I'm sure you're waiting for me to regale you with details of my figure eights, camel spins and spirals, but alas, I have no such story. I skated straight forward, stiff as a board, arms out for balance. My routine was to go around the rink two times and back up the ramp, take off my skates, find my dollar for a snack, sit by the fire and watch the clock till Mom returned.

When I was a teen I tried to ski. It was the '60s and maybe I had a whiff of someone's marijuana. What other reason could cause me to *choose* to go out on a steep slope with oversized Popsicle sticks attached to my feet and try to conquer nature by careening down hills named Devil's Dive, Suicide Slide, and Mountain of No Return?

I guess I was trying to impress my boyfriend, and hey, he married me despite the fact that on my first trip up Nosebleed Hill I was too terrified to get off the chair lift. For those of you that have not risked your life on a chair lift, the object is that you jump off at the top as it whips around the corner, taking you with it if you don't get off in time. Do you know how embarrassing it is to miss that spot? Well, I do. They have to stop the lift at the bottom to let you off.

The only good thing about skiing that I could discern was that there was a reward if I skied to the bottom in one piece—the reward was that I could take off my skis, park them outside (I always hoped someone would steal them, but no such luck) and sit in the chalet drinking hot chocolate while I waited for my toes to defrost, which is the most painful experience in the world, bar none. And yes, I have had a baby. This is worse.

My sister-in-law invited us to go snowmobiling once. That couldn't be too bad, right? Their routine was to stop at about 50 saloons along the trail to "warm up." Well, that's all well and good, but after a toddy at the first bar and a toddy at the second and a toddy at the third, one thing becomes clear—you cannot get out of those snowmobile suits fast enough to make it to the bathroom. As I said, we only joined them once.

Good friends talked us into trying cross country skiing. Simple enough. No terrifying downhill plunges, no bouncing over a mogul so hard it sends you airborne for five minutes, no ice crystals freezing your eyelids shut.

Things were going fairly well until we came to a hill with a one percent grade. Unable to manage even that, I fell upside down into the snow bank with my feet in the air (where else are they going to be with skis on them?). I looked and felt like a turtle. My husband and friends were less than helpful because they couldn't stop laughing long enough to right me, and my futile attempts to overturn myself only made them laugh harder.

When my daughter was ten I thought it would be fun to buy snow shoes for each of us. I put them under the tree at midnight on Christmas Eve disguised as a family present from Santa. At dawn on Christmas morning I woke, looked out at the snow, checked the thermometer, opened my daughter's room to see her still asleep, raced to the tree, grabbed the snowshoes and ran to the attic where I hid them so my family would never know of my lapse in judgment. What was I thinking? Snowshoeing involves being outdoors. The day after Christmas I got in line with the other returners of unwanted items. So much for that fun, family winter adventure I had envisioned. Bah Humbug!

Yes, my experiences with snow have not been peachy, and I don't care if snowmen can come to life, I won't be out there making one. I've had three fender benders involving snow; none of them my fault, of course. I have slipped on the ice and broken my elbow. I have had my car stuck in a snow bank, had to shovel my way out of my driveway, and had to scrape ice from my windshield.

And what of snow's less glamorous siblings; slush and sleet and blizzards and frost and—oh, never mind—it's too dismal to think about. My apologies to those of you who like winter sports and winter weather and winter wonderlands. All I can say to you people is this: can you spell A-R-I Z-O-N-A?

Missive On Christmas Letters

So, it's almost that time of year again. Sleigh bells and whiskers on kittens and warm woolen mittens and all that good stuff. I need to get my Christmas letter written, copied, and out to the masses waiting patiently for it to arrive in their mailboxes, both physical and virtual.

What can I say this year that sounds different from last year? If I wait a few more weeks, maybe I can just start next year's letter early. I had better look at previous correspondence to remind myself of all the good times from years past.

Let's see, there's the draft where I mentioned that I had crashed the car (never stating in so many words that I was putting on my lipstick at the time). Aaaah, and another where I admit to lusting after the milkman. That one never made it to the final copy. I can't forget the year I went on for three paragraphs about how Jim had retired and I was still trudging through five feet of snow to get to my office each day. I'm sure that probably made my family and friends think…well, I don't want to know what they thought.

Of course, I can report that Jim and I did have some super times over the years. When Ann graduated from kindergarten we made her a cake. When Ann graduated from 8th grade we threw her a party. When Ann graduated from high school we took her to Europe. When Ann graduated from college, we gave her a car. When Ann got her Master's in California, we took her to Europe again. Yup, Jim and I sure did a lot of cool stuff—no wonder we're filing for Chapter 11 next week.

Of course, there have been sad times, too, like when our cat Leo bit the dust. And when our seven-year-old roof was flawed and we got nothing from the insurance company. I could write about falling off of our jet ski and deciding my husband could have all that jet ski fun by himself. We all know by now that my forte is shopping—I rarely fall down and I never get wet. Or, I could let everyone know that the dozens of books I read last summer required me to sit constantly, which in turn caused my rear end to spread to gigantic proportions. I'm sticking with that reason, come hell or high water.

Don't you love the Christmas letters you receive from friends and family? You know, the ones where they regurgitate all the wonderful times they had with Tom, Dick, and Harry? One letter will state that the writer's adorable granddaughter won a tennis tournament for four-year-olds, accompanied by a picture that shows the child holding a trophy three times bigger than she is. Some of us would just like to have a grandchild and promise never to bore anyone with pictures—unless you bring it up of course, in which case I'll have a photo album or two handy.

And then there's Great Aunt Alice from northern Minnesota who writes that all of her nieces and nephews visited her last year. Of course they did—she's filthy rich. And I'm sure you have all received the one about how the sender's brother's wife's sister's son's mother-in-law's best friend's cousin's daughter's second child from her first marriage just won the Nobel Prize for chemistry or needlepointing.

I wonder what my mother would have written about me if Christmas letters had been popular back in the days of yore? "Whew, it was close. Bonnie barely graduated from high school. Luckily there was one schleppy student that had a lower GPA. We bribed her way into a convent which was the only place we felt she could achieve even a modicum of success. We do worry about her being a model nun because she already has two children out of wedlock and lately started smoking that Mary-J-Wanna."

Rocky Road is Not Just an Ice Cream

Maybe this should be our letter this year?

Hello Family and Friends,

Well, here we are in sunny Arizona. We'd like to say we miss you, but we don't. Heard you're having terrible snow storms in Minnesota. It would be impossible for us to care any less than we already do. We know some of you are waiting to be invited to our desert hacienda, but that'll never happen.

As intrigued as you must be to catch up on our lives, you can only guess at how inspired we are to share it with you. Let's see, I look the same (darn) and I feel the same (yea) and when I look over at Jim snoozing in the chair, I think he's pretty much the same, too. It's just been a delightful blur of retirement-based exhilaration all winter. Let the senior citizen merriment continue! The whirlwind of parties start at 4 p.m. and are in full swing till, oh, gosh, probably 6:30. Yep, yep, we are livin' the dream.

Also, we live vicariously through our daughter and son-in-law's glamorous big-city life. Not that we really have a handle on what big-city life entails, but it sounds exciting to us. They often travel to various ports-of-call and all we get are some picture postcards. Not one invite to join them on their glamorous adventures. We're sure it's just an oversight.

We just want to remind you again that we are in a lovely, sandy paradise and you are in freezing, icy, cold, snowy, dark Minnesota. Na na na na na and Merry Christmas.

Affectionately,
Bonnie and Jim

Dear Mrs. Claus

Dear Mrs. Claus

Can we talk? It occurred to me that if I want to get my wishes fulfilled, I need to go directly to the Boss, the Big Cheese, the Head Honcho. In other words, the woman behind the man. I don't mean to complain, especially around Christmas time, but Santa has not been living up to his promises.

I distinctly remember writing a letter two years ago asking him to make my extra weight go away. What did he do? He sent me a recumbent bike. I'm thinking that he was so preoccupied with other requests that he just wasn't thinking clearly. It's okay, I understand and forgive him.

However, last year I schlepped down to the mall, stood in line with a million other devotees and sat on your husband's lap. We had a nice conversation. He asked me what I wanted and I told him diamonds look really good on me. That's what I said; rewind the tape and check if you don't believe me. What I found under the tree was Liz Taylor's White Diamonds perfume. I really thought I'd made myself clear, but I know it was noisy with all those kids in line; some of them shouting at me to hurry up. I feel I've had a fairly long relationship with your hubby. After all, we go back all the way from when I was four years old. You can understand why I think I deserved some extra time. And by the way, do give him my apologies for the knee injury I caused him.

There is just a teensy tiny other issue I'd like to bring to your attention. Why did Santa forget to bring me the hybrid golf clubs I asked for? Don't get me wrong, I did appreciate the box of pink golf balls. With the economy the way it is, I can see how gifts for everyone in the world can get pretty expensive, but still, he could have warned me and saved me the money I spent on the exclusive golf membership at the beach side country club. I did notice he drew blood when he bit his lip, so maybe the knee pain was overriding any response from him at the moment.

Mrs. Claus—may I call you Sandy—I was wondering if maybe your husband mentioned me in past years? I was the one who wanted a real, live reindeer when I was eight, and an actual train caboose to use as a play house when I was ten, a white stallion named Lightning when I was twelve, and the boy down the street when I was fourteen. And then, when I was sixteen, I made the mistake of not writing to him, and yikes, was that a Christmas morning disaster! I haven't made that faux pas again. I believe that Santa can do anything, but he might need a little guidance, so please, Sandy, could you put in a good word for me?

I'll send you cookies and my super-secret recipe for eggnog spinach anchovy bread. It's kind of a time consuming baking project, though. I'm guessing that's why my friends and relatives beg me not to make it for them—they don't want me to work too hard.

So, in closing, I just want you to know that this year I'm asking your husband for a winning lottery ticket and the ability to touch my toes by Easter. Heck, I'd settle for just seeing my toes by Easter! Matter of fact, if he could just arrange for me to know that my toes are still attached, I'd be very grateful. That's all. Please feel free to write to me at bonniewillemssen@gmail.com

Sincerely, Bonnie

Dear Bonnie,

You are correct. You have left a very lasting impression on everyone at the North Pole, Santa and the elves alike. My husband says to tell you that after his knee surgery and seven months of therapy, he is much better. He promises he will make sure all your wishes come true. I am thrilled to tell you that he is going to send you a 1999 Pennsylvania lottery ticket; it was worth two million dollars to the winner and he knows how thrilled you will be to frame it. Also, after much discussion and contemplation, he is taking my suggestion and bringing you a long-handled mirror which will make seeing your toes so much easier. So don't feel it's necessary to sit on his lap at the mall again. And there's definitely no need to send those cookies or that, ah, interesting *bread recipe. We both hope you have a wonderful 2012.*

Best wishes,
Sandy

Dear Santa,

It occurs to me that I have been blaming the wrong person for my misinterpreted gift requests…my apologies.

Merry Christmas,
Bonnie

Hippy, Hippy New Year

My dieting saga started with the New Year. Not New Year's Day, of course. That would be a ridiculous time to start a diet. No, I decided to start on January 2nd. Of course, January 2nd arrived and there were a lot of leftovers to eat up. On top of that, my husband announced it was Rose Bowl Monday, and everyone knows you can't watch a football game without snacks and a beverage of your choice. So, with practiced ease, I procrastinated until Tuesday. I'm sharing this story with you so you don't fall into the same pitfalls and perils I have.

Here are some suggestions: first, you need to cleanse your house of any tempting snacks—I suggest eating them slowly. Enjoy the luscious and silky texture of the Lindt chocolate one last time, savor the spiciness of the pepperoni on your final pizza, and salivate over the salty goodness of a bag of Cheetos. Notice I didn't say *last* bag of Cheetos; after all, the diet gurus say *be realistic*.

Start your weight loss program by making a list of *why* you want to lose weight. My list has things on it like: I want to lose weight so that I can power walk to the donut shop; I want to lose weight so that the grocery boys will quit calling me ma'am; and I want to lose weight so that George Clooney will ask me to be his date for the Oscars.

I'm sure you have lots of your own ideas. Wait, we're not done with lists. You need to make a list of what you can and cannot eat. I call mine the "Can and Cannot Eat List." Topping my column of approved foods are potatoes—they're a veggie and it's not my fault if they slice them, fry them, salt them and put them in a bag of irresistible crunch. Carmel apples are next, followed closely by candied yams, and so forth and so on, right on down to chocolate covered raisins. Oh wait, I think I had to put the raisins in the *other* column.

Next, make a list of all the things that will happen if you lose weight. Here's mine:

1. No more shopping in the super big mama department.
2. No more having the fire department on standby to hoist me out of the tub.
3. No more wanting to shoot my friends when they say they're too full for seconds.
4. No more having the cashier at McDonalds look behind me quizzically when I order eight happy meals.

Need I go on?

When the big day, January 3rd, arrived, I had two scales ready and calibrated. One weighed *me*, the other weighed my *food*. Try not to get them mixed up. I had a sheet of paper with two columns; one for my food choices and one for the calories. I ate my first item of the day—a banana. I wrote it down. B-A-N-A-N-A. Darn, 90 calories. I was only going to allow myself 500 calories a day till I got to my goal.

The banana was gone in a flash. Maybe I should have mashed it up and eaten it with a baby spoon. Despite my inability to make the yummy yellow fruit last more than a few seconds, I was feeling surprisingly good! Peppy, psyched and ready to take on the world! *I can do this*, I told myself. When the first hunger pang hit, I ignored it. The second followed and I thought, okay, I'll have whole wheat toast. I was delighted with myself for choosing something healthy. I wrote it down like a good girl.

Rocky Road is Not Just an Ice Cream

Accountability is key, you know. At least, that's what that Diet Diva told me last summer when I went to the nutrition clinic. As if she, a 90-pound munchkin, had ever tried squeezing a size-20 tush into size-18 jeans. She counseled me to *listen* to my body. I took it as sound advice, and did as she asked. What I actually heard, though, was my body screaming for Butterfingers and Doritos.

A sadist if ever there was one, she told me I should never "officially" diet, just make good choices, cut portions and exercise more. But hey, if I knew how to make good choices I wouldn't have had to see her in the first place.

Do you know how long an afternoon is when you've only had carrots and celery at lunch? I ate at the crack of noon, and by 12:30 wished I had eaten more. By 1:00 I was convinced a small bite of something could easily serve as a well-deserved reward for my stoic and epically long battle against hunger. At 1:30, having held off valiantly, I mentally trashed the acceptable foods on my list. 2:00 was hard. I was almost too weak to get off the couch and make my way to the pantry for a little look-see.

Around 2:30 I was famished—it had been, like, decades since lunch. Seeing stars, my life flashing before my eyes and ready to expire from lack of food, I managed to make it to the freezer to grab a carton of ice cream. Remembering my goal to be accountable, I wrote down the calories in pencil just in case I had to erase to make room for a more acceptable entry. I justified my quick fix as being squarely in the dairy category. And, I was no longer fainting from hunger. The Oreo chaser I had after the ice cream may have helped with that. I decided to skip the nap I was contemplating, and the rest of the afternoon passed without incident.

Supper was a homemade concoction of veggie soup, brown rice with grilled chicken and various other *healthy* choices. My husband, wanting to be supportive, ate the same foods I did. He lost 22 pounds on the first day, and I for some reason gained 2. Go figure. I've heard people say that when you're dieting it's important to take it one day at a time.

Convinced of what a superb idea that is, the second day of my diet will be, let's see...how about March 9th?

(AUTHOR'S DISCLAIMER: THESE DIETING TIPS ARE NOT APPROVED BY ANY ORGANIZATION KNOWN TO MANKIND, NOR WILL THEY WORK IF TRIED.)

Like Sands through the Hourglass

Oh goodie, January has arrived and I'm still not sure what my New Year's resolutions should be. Should I go the regular route?

1. To lose weight I vow never to eat again.
2. To improve my mind I vow to give up TV.
3. I vow to stay in better contact with my friends and family so I can find out the latest gossip, I mean, ah, so I can keep the family spirit alive. That's it.
4. I vow to brush my teeth three times a day, floss, and scrape my tongue religiously so that I'll never have to wear dentures.
5. I vow to jog 20 miles every day so that I can have buns of steel—or steel wool, whichever comes first.

Don't stare. You can see I didn't keep any of those past resolutions, although I did get some great family gossip.

I was kind of hoping to sleep through January. That way, by the time I woke up I could just say that it wasn't worth starting any resolutions. I've tried to sleep soundly, but my husband keeps waking me up to tell me I'm snoring, so that plan didn't work out as well as I'd hoped.

Now I'm scrambling to come up with something, anything, to resolve not to do this year. Here's an easy one—I resolve to never get on my husband's jet ski again after that graceful dip I took in the cold, numbing waters of the mighty Mississippi. In the subsequent hour it took me to pull myself back up on the jet ski, I had visions of my toes encountering a snapping turtle, a six-foot catfish, or the shark from *Jaws*.

I definitely resolve never to ride a bike through a tunnel again. That ended up with me face-down in cold, mucky water with the bike on top of me. And that brings to mind another don't—canoeing. The Kickapoo River winds and weaves through glacial rocks and farmlands, always maintaining a moderate depth of about three feet. When our friends overturned, my husband jumped out of our canoe to help them. He left me in the canoe, rudderless. I drifted into tree roots on the bend.

Once there, I also jumped out to help. Who knew that at the bend the water is 25 feet deep? Luckily for my husband, the water flowing over my head turned all the swear words coming out of my mouth into incomprehensible burbles. No more canoeing.

At Christmas, not dispirited in the least by my less than sterling record of turning the ordinary into the bizarre, we went horseback riding. I know the corners of your mouth are already twitching; you're stifling the laugh that is begging to come out. Shame on you for even thinking that my experience on the horse's ass was amusing.

It wasn't the fact that my horse, Buttercup, looked pleadingly at the trail leader when he saw me, nor was it the fact that he paid no attention to me and raced back to the stable in record time. No, none of that was a problem; it was the fact that it took six cowhands to get me off the horse that determined that I would not be joining the rodeo anytime soon.

And even though I haven't tried bronco roping, hang-gliding, or race car driving, I think that perhaps I'm not cut out for anything quite so robust. So my only New Year's resolution for this year will be to sit on the davenport and read, getting up only now and then to get a snack from the pantry and refill my glass of bourbon.

The Magic of Memories

Yup, it's officially here. Sirius radio has two channels already playing Christmas carols. The stores have sold the last of their Halloween goodies and crowded out Thanksgiving items in favor of full-fledged trees decked out for the holidays. Sales people are starting to wish their customers the politically correct "Happy Holidays," and the aromatic dispenser in the ladies' restroom at Macy's is puffing out cranberry or pine.

People all around me make the same tired complaints. "Seems Christmas is coming earlier every year." "What's with these stores? It's practically still the Fourth of July." And then they turn to me for agreement, but I don't agree. I couldn't possibly agree any less. I *love* Christmas! More than any holiday *I love Christmas*.

I have a good friend that literally worships Halloween. She has two-and-a-half trillion Halloween decorations, she has annual Halloween parties; she is so into Halloween that I'm pretty sure she secretly practices Wicca. Another friend is thrilled with the family Thanksgiving tradition. Nothing is allowed to change—tons of family, tons of turkey, tons of laughter and love. That's all well and good, but it's not Christmas.

I have fond memories of my mom serving oyster stew on Christmas Eve every year. I never ate it, but I definitely learned to appreciate oyster *crackers*. I don't know what she let me eat instead, but whatever it was, I was glad. Only after the dishes were done would we open the family presents.

I thought I'd burst from the waiting. It was so very special and I'll always be grateful for the magic my mother infused into Christmas. My dad, on the other hand, had no clue about the magic of Christmas—he only worried himself sick about whether the Christmas tree was getting too dry, and never, but *never* was the fireplace ever to be burning without an adult in the room.

However, he did have his traditions, too. Each year he would put two envelopes on the branches of the tree. They had money in them—100 dollars for my mom and 25 for me. I think I remember that as the years passed he increased the amounts, but I do think of those envelopes fondly, especially the year he made a mistake and reversed our names.

When I was a little girl, my dad brought home the most innovative and marvelous toy—a battery operated donkey. You pushed a button and the donkey walked. It was attached to a cord that provided the juice. I was sure it was a magic donkey and it kept me enthralled for weeks. You didn't have to plug it in; you just pushed a button. The only warranty on that donkey was my dad's stern warning that I shouldn't use it too often because it would eventually stop working. Apparently they didn't have replacement batteries back in yesteryear.

Yes, life was simpler then—no one whined when the new basketball deflated, no one cried if the shiny colors wore off the jacks, no one whimpered when a roller broke off a skate. It was kaput till Mom or Dad decided to buy you another one. Gifts for no reason were unheard of. There were only two times a year you got gifts—your birthday and Christmas.

Hurting people's feeling by returning a present was nconceivable and downright *preposterous*. It didn't matter if Grandma Jane's gift of an olive-drab and puce sweater was the ugliest thing that ever hung on a human body, or that the new bathrobe was the worst shade of salmon to ever disgrace a crayon box. It was yours to keep, wear, use, or abuse for a year. You didn't trade it in, you didn't make a face and roll your eyes and say things like, "I asked for a Wii, not a Winnie the Pooh."

Mother insisted on flocked trees for several years in a row. It wasn't until the year she got a pink flocked tree that my dad finally convinced her to stick with a plain old green tree. No way did she even consider an artificial tree. I loved multicolored lights. With each flocked tree she would have matching lights; a blue flocked tree called for blue lights, a red flocked tree called for red lights and so forth, but, when she settled on natural trees again she went with multicolored lights.

We could only light them when we were all in the room (my dad again), and so I'd wait patiently for her to finish the dishes and my dad to finish shoveling the snow or doing his bills, and then they would finally come in the living room and turn on the tree. Unfortunately, Mom always put blue lights on our outside trees. That practice very much disappointed me. All-blue lights didn't seem enough like Christmas.

Dad owned an office supply store in our hometown, and there was a music store next to his. I begged for the new Chipmunks' Christmas 45 record one year. He promised he would bring it home for me. When he came through the door that night at 5:50 on the dot, I was waiting for that record. I saw his empty hands and he saw my face. He turned around, got back in the car, and drove the three miles back downtown to his store where he had left it. He was a kind man. As Dean Martin used to croon, "Memories are made of this."

*Section 4: Love and Marriage -
or why didn't I get all that cool stuff when I got married?*

What's In a Name?

My daughter lives with her boyfriend, and my husband and I have a problem. No, we aren't against the relationship; we're fine with her choices. She is pretty, smart and fun—who wouldn't want to live with her? We're glad she moved out; isn't every parent relieved when their child doesn't want to live with them forever?

We have a different problem. What do we call this man that has stolen our daughter's heart? We don't know how to describe him when we tell people about them. If Ann and Erik are coming for a visit, we don't know who to say is visiting. Our daughter and her boyfriend? Her comrade? Her *sidekick*? Doesn't boyfriend seem kind of highschoolish? She might like the term soul mate, and with her love of shoes, a *sole* mate might be even better. She's had boyfriends since she was 14 and none of them invited her to move in with them, so we have no experience with name calling.

Okay, we've perhaps done some *name calling* but it was in reference to a different topic. We could call him her significant other, but that sounds so impersonal. Calling him her roommate doesn't quite cover the sleeping arrangements, at least, not the roommates I had back in my day. Of course, today there are friends with benefits, but, excuse me, there's no way I'm introducing him that way. What about bedfellow? Not a chance, that makes me think of that old movie with Rock Hudson and Gig Young. I thought pseudo son-in-law had a nice ring, but my husband put the nix to that, so I vehemently nixed his suggestion of spousal equivalent. Not daunted in the least, he then suggested life partner, but I think that's the preferred term for gay couples. My Mah Jongg friends thought future baby daddy had a nice ring. I can't say I don't like it, but who knows if it will ever be true. Potential father of our grandchildren takes way too long to say.

So, there you have it. What do we call him? *He who shall remain nameless* is only for Harry Potter fans. If I mention we're going to drive out to see Ann and Erik, people will ask, "Who's Erik? Her fiancé? Her husband?" Alas, neither of those terms seems to loom on the horizon yet. Why can't life be simple? There should be a word for this man that lives with our daughter. Person of interest? Man of the hour? Bosom buddy? Wolf in sheep's clothing? Best man? Bachelor Number One? I guess we'll just say he's the "live in." But, wait a minute. *She's* the "live in." It's his house. Oh, dear, maybe we need to figure out what to call our daughter.

Let Me Call You Sweetheart

Valentine's Day. Broken hearts. Candy kisses. The highs and lows of anticipation and disappointment. In grade school I looked for a valentine from everyone in my class. In high school I hoped for a rose and a mushy card, and in college I wished that my true love would ask me to marry him and live in a big mansion. It never happened, but eventually I found my Valentine. His name is Jim. We've been together for a *long* time. Come this spring my sweetheart and I will have been married 40 years.

I guess we bucked the trend and upheld our vows to stay together through sleet and snow and rain…oh wait, that's a different vow. And what about those lovey-dovey valentine gifts? Well, let's just say he manages to get me something wonderful—once every decade or so.

I still remember my wedding day, which is fortunate because my memory lapses are getting worse. Yes, I recall I was a young, beautiful, incredibly smart girl (my memory is impeccable when it comes to *certain* details) who was marrying the man of her dreams. Well, at least a man who was willing to marry me.

As I stood at the front of the church, my dad leaned over and said, "It's not too late to back out." Yikes! Don't tell me this now, Dad. I was already totally uncertain if I was doing the right thing. Was this the right man? "And the final Jeopardy answer is: Bonnie and Jim Willemssen." "Alex, the question is: Who is still married after 40 years?"

We began our married life with single digit incomes and thought we were on top of the world. We drove a 1968 red Volkswagen Beetle, lived close to our respective jobs, had an adequate apartment and most of our family lived close by. I was an elementary teacher, so I had the summer off. I set up housekeeping, just like when I was a little girl pretending to be all grown up. The ironing board goes here, the breadbox goes there, and the little miniature plates go on the table for when papa doll gets home from that place called *work*.

In that first year of marital bliss, I wore an apron. An *apron*! Can you imagine? It had yellow chickens on it and blended perfectly with my avocado appliances and my yellow, orange and green curtains, which in turn matched my linoleum floor and Formica countertop. Despite the fact that I didn't know how to cook, life was good. With only one car, I had to get up five minutes before my dear husband (we were newlyweds then, so I still called him dear) and drive him to work.

One time I got stopped for speeding (I was very intent on getting back to bed quickly), thank Heaven the cop never noticed I was wearing my robe and slippers. Feeling lucky to have avoided a ticket for indecent exposure, I decided in the future to slip a trench coat over my nightgown for those early morning chauffeuring duties, and I traded my pink fuzzy slippers for flip flops, which in those days were called thongs. Nowadays if I said I wore my thongs you would think this was a different story entirely.

We forgot to have kids for six years, and then suddenly it occurred to us that maybe we should produce an heir, which in our case turned out to be an heiress. She was sweet and adorable and made our lives complete, right up till the time she learned to talk. Oh boy! Did she take after me? No! Well, in one small way—we both have a way with words. Did she take after her father? Darn tootin'! Two of them, oh my Lord, there were *two* of them. The good news is that if something happens to my better half, I have another one to step in and take care of me.

Yes, living and learning has been interesting. Jim learned to pick up the phone and call the insurance company when I would come home after another fender bender, he learned to balance the checkbook after I

Rocky Road is Not Just an Ice Cream

was through balancing the checkbook, and he also learned to deal with my mother—an impressive feat that even I never quite mastered. I learned to put gas in the car, start the snow blower and program the VCR. We now understand each other's pointing, mumbling, grunting and head nods. I know my sweetheart's limitations, so I save him lots of time by ordering my own red roses and sending myself a mushy Valentine.

Let me call you sweetheart, I'm in love with you
Just keep the checkbook balanced, and I won't say boo
Keep the money solvent in our joint account
I will call you sweetheart if it's the right amount

Here Comes the Mother of the Bride

I've known for a while that my daughter is getting married in the spring. The whole first month after A-Day (Announcement Day) I dieted, and yet I *gained* three pounds. I redoubled my efforts for the second month and gained three more pounds—and now I know what "redoubling" means.

Obviously the scale wasn't going in the direction I wanted it to go, so I scoured diet books, change-your-life books, mental-adjustment books, and self-help books in search of wisdom and guidance. It might have been more beneficial for me to just get off my duff and exercise instead. For years I've been telling people I have a slow metabolism, or there is a good chance that I'm Kate Smith reincarnated (if you don't get that reference you are too young to read my column).

I tell people that the likeliest culprit of my inability to shed pounds is that I'm part of a space alien experiment in which ET has implanted a FAT CHIP in my brain to prevent me from losing weight no matter what I do. So while NASA tries to figure out a way to remove the chip that ALF implanted, I have to deal with the consequences of my lazy ways.

Horror of horrors, I had to break down and finally look for a mother-of-the-bride dress for *this* body, which is not the body that I envisioned I would be shopping for. No, the body that was going to walk down the aisle at my daughter's wedding was going to look like Suzanne Somers. Not going to happen. *C'est la vie.* And hello, do you have any idea what it's like to try on dresses that don't zip up, don't pull up, don't pull

Rocky Road is Not Just an Ice Cream

down, don't stretch out and don't cover my fluffy arms, thunder thighs, beach ball tummy, or my derriere (which is actually quite small when you compare it to something like, oh, Montana)?

I was getting so desperate for a dress, I was starting to check out REI, Gander Mountain, and the local tent and awning shop. Yes, it's just a joy to have the salesclerk crowd into the dressing room with you to "help" push and shove your girth into the gray and pink satin number that makes you look like a whale going to the prom or the pink tulle and lace getup that practically shouts *hippos* from Disney's *Fantasia*.

The sales lady's comments ran along these lines: "You look glowing in that, dear." "Oh now, you're a large woman and should be proud of it". "No one notices the jiggle under your arms, really." And my favorite—"All eyes will be on the bride." What? Everyone isn't going to be looking at me? Well, who knew? In that case I can wear that purple dress I bought for the Red Hat Club 20 years ago. Actually, I can't because I gave it to Goodwill.

In a last ditch attempt to find the one store in the whole valley that sells *chunky chic* wedding clothes, I had to drive to the big city. Not being all that familiar with the streets and alleys of the aforementioned big city, my girlfriend accompanied me on my dire quest.

Luckily, she has a teeny-tiny guy who lives inside her car that has a phone book on his lap 24/7. She called him every hour to have him look up the address of the next mother-of-the-bride store. I think his name is Ahn Starr. I'm not sure what my friend pays him, but how much could he possibly need living inside her dash board?

So, I found a dress. It covers me from stem to stern, from hull to helm, and in keeping with the nautical references, I probably look like the Titanic. At least it was my size—*super big mama*—and as an added bonus I could actually purchase it at the store and bring it home with me. In most bridal shops you have to order the dress, and you can't return it if it doesn't fit, but they *will* be happy to alter it for you—for an extravagant fee. One owner told me it was mine to wear, give away, sell, or throw.

And have you checked the prices of mother-of-the-bride dresses? What makes a dress cost so much in a bridal shop and a fraction of that price at Macy's? Back in 1972 my wedding dress cost a whopping 100 dollars and this week I bought *shoes* for 100 dollars! Golly, how prices have changed over the past 40 years. Did I mention that our anniversary is the day after our daughter's wedding? We get a son-in-law for an anniversary present. Don't get me wrong, he's super great, but dear daughter, would a Mediterranean cruise have really cost so much, or a new BMW? Or maybe just a simple hot tub?

In conclusion, it took me 60 *days* to shop for my wedding outfit. It took my husband 60 *minutes* to pick out his. We walked into the men's shop. He tried on three suits. He picked one. He had the tailor measure it. We charged it. We left. Next wedding he gets to wear the satin gown and I'll wear the suit and tie.

To Have and To Hold

Most of you know that we recently attended our daughter's wedding. I had little control over any of it, so I wasn't sure what to expect, but it was perfect from start to finish. Well, Jim and I did have that car accident on the way to the wedding rehearsal, but no one was hurt, and so other than that all was great. Oh, and I did fall in the tub the day of the wedding, but I survived. Besides, who needs (or wants) to be able to dance all night?

And I guess I should mention that silly little thing where one of the crystal goblets shattered on impact as we toasted each other, but, you know, other than that, it was all perfect. There is another thing, though. I know it seems like the poor dead horse has been beaten enough, but did it really have to rain on *that* day only? Friday and Sunday were 80 degrees and sunny, but Saturday had to be rainy, windy, and cool. Aside from all that, it was a fairy tale wedding with a bride that looked like Grace Kelly and a groom that embodied Prince Charming.

I know I'm the mother-of-the-bride, but, really, it's true as tapioca, they looked spectacular. They chose to get married in a vineyard in Virginia. The alliteration kind of rolls off the tongue, doesn't it? We had vino in a vineyard in Virginia. Well, I didn't have vino 'cause I'm a teetotaler, but as the father-of-the-bride can attest after paying the bar bill, everyone enjoyed the vino a lot.

Our daughter, who wouldn't touch peas when she was a child, is now a gourmet cook and chose foods for the wedding with words like artisanal goat cheese (personally, I'm not sure I would like the same cheese as a goat), dill pollen (which I'm sure you need to take an antihistamine for), capers (I like mine in a murder mystery), antipasta (I don't think people should be against pasta), foie gras (I think that fake grass just looks tacky), and how about words like coriander, truffle oil, organic garlic, red onion confit, fennel and aji dolce peppers; none of which I have a clue about nor can I pronounce.

I latched onto the only word I could figure out—shrimp—and Jim and I enjoyed a shrimp something or other with this and that and a dash of such and such and it was good despite my misgivings. Others seemed to be enjoying the food and many raved about it to us, so I guess those in the know (Jim and I are not part of the "in the know" crowd) loved the selections. All I can say is thank God she didn't serve something like octopus medallions or sushi bouillabaisse; not that I've had them, nor am I positive they exist, but they sound dreadful.

What did I end up wearing you might want to know? Well, even if you don't, I'm telling you anyway. I found a black ensemble that covered me from my triple chins to my puffy ankles in opaque blackness with a modicum of lighter colors added in the jacket so that I didn't blend totally into the night sky. I spruced it up with gold shoes and purse, dangled some jewelry around the appropriate places on my body (not my navel or nose) and slapped on some make-up, and voila! I was presentable. Actually, no one knew I was alive with all eyes on the glowing bride, so I shouldn't have worried about what I wore.

I had to give an impromptu speech at the rehearsal dinner. So, unplanned, unprepared and unexpected as it was, I managed to rattle on for 15 minutes, keeping everyone in stitches with stories about Ann and her dad. I was standing in front of the dessert table. Do you have any idea how hard it was to concentrate with Georgia pecan cheesecake, truffle torte, chocolate fudge cake and tiramisu calling to me? Moses would have given up the tablets if he had seen those sugary delights. Jimmy Carter would have lusted *outside* his heart and Johnny Cash would have written an ode to the display of decadence.

The week ended as it began. Jim and I packed our SUV to the brim with stuff. On the drive out, the clothes for all the wedding events were laid in the back and carefully kept wrinkle free. On the way home again everything was rolled in a ball in the suitcases, necessitated by a need for space for the things Ann wanted to get out of her house so she could make room for the wonderful new wedding items they had received.

For a minute I thought we were back on her college campus loading the van from seats to sunroof with all the essentials a girl needs for a few months away from home—TV, clothes, computer, clothes, CD/DVD player, clothes, cell phone, clothes, guitar, clothes, microwave, clothes, electric toothbrush, clothes, checkbook and clothes. On that note, I'm opening a resale shop to defray the cost of the wedding.

Trust Me

Picture this: it's 1972 and my new husband wants to impress me with his waterskiing skills by doing a snap-start off the dock on one ski. I'm sure it worked perfectly many times before, but this was not one of those times. He broke his neck.

"Are you all right?" I cried.

"Not sure yet," he answered.

I cheerfully suggested that he go take a hot shower. "You'll feel much better—*trust me*." Later, at the hospital, when they strapped him to a gurney with sandbags on either side of his head, the doctor explained that if he had taken that shower he would have been paralyzed when his stiff muscles relaxed.

Jump to 2001. Jim wanted us to join the hiking club. At our first meeting they explained the rules. I was appalled to hear that there were no flushing toilets along the trails. Worse, we were expected to carry out the paper we used if we did *you know what*. Carry it out? Are they kidding? As if it couldn't have gotten any worse, potty breaks were mandated by the leader—men on one side of the hill, women on the other, but no stop sign to keep other hikers from bounding over the hill to behold our exposed bottoms.

Squatting behind a tiny cactus is never a stellar idea in my book on any given day. I'm all for bonding with my environment, if my environment encompasses the pure and pristine atmosphere of Nordstrom's, Tiffany's, and The Cheese Cake Factory. However, Jim decided hiking was for him. After the first trip he returned limping, thinking he should go to the doctor.

"You're fine," I said. "You just strained some muscles. But if you really want to go see the doctor we'll go to the emergency ward, but you better act like this is a real emergency 'cause *trust me*, it's nothing." A few hours, doctors, and x-rays later, Jim was scheduled for knee replacement surgery.

A couple years ago Jim asked me to look at his upper arm. "Do you see anything?" he demanded with worry in his voice.

Dutiful wife that I am, I studied the nonexistent spot, gave a stately nod and said, "Well, you better call the dermatologist." Under my breath I mumbled something about mountains and molehills (pardon the intended pun), but I'm pretty sure he didn't hear me in his mad dash to get to the phone.

As appointments go, it wasn't too long to wait (a few months), but in three weeks he wanted me to check out the miniscule freckle again. "I think it's changed," he asserted.

With lips clamped tightly so as to hold back the uncivil words that were dying to blurt out, I examined the area he was indicating. "So, call the doctor and ask to get in earlier," I suggested, trying to match my concern with his. "I'm sure it's fine. *Trust me*." The following week, the doctor removed the melanoma in my husband's arm.

Fast forward. The local heart hospital was offering a discount on a noninvasive scan that detected heart problems. I made an appointment for myself. As I hung up the phone, my husband returned from his two-hour exercise routine. When I told him what I had done he asked, "Did you make an appointment for me?"

"Why in the world would I make an appointment for you?" Swearing under my breath about the money for his appointment being better spent on things for me, I called the hospital again. On the day of the appointment I was fearful of what they would certainly find wrong with my heart. After the tests, we were told we'd be called ASAP if there were any immediate concerns after the doctors read the tests. I went home and packed my overnight bag and waited by the phone, certain I would be called to come in immediately for quadruple triple double bypass surgery.

No call came. I was still waiting two weeks later when Jim felt jaw pain. It was pretty obvious to me that he had an ear infection. Jim called his doctor who said that jaw pain was a symptom of a heart attack and to go to the emergency ward right away. Well, that was the silliest thing I had ever heard. How could Jim, the guy who got up at 6 a.m. to do hours of cardio and weight lifting, who ate healthy, who never smoked and didn't drink, have a bum ticker?

I don't think so! I dragged him around with me all day running errands. Finally, I noticed he looked flushed and sweaty. I ascertained that he was only thinking of the money I was spending—a scary prospect for him on any given day. "You probably just have a bad cold, but I'm sure you'll be fine. *Trust me.*"

Before the day was done, we were at the emergency ward. When the doctor came to share the results of the blood tests, I was prepared to say "See, I told you so," and take Jim home, but the doctor, apparently not able to read my mind, instead said, "You have had a heart attack." The next day they put a stent in his blocked artery, which was blocked by no less than 100 percent.

So, what has my hubby learned after all these years? Well, for one, don't listen to me for Pete's sake! You probably think he should start checking Match.com for a new wife. Oh, by the way, I'm available for advice and medical consultations. After all, I've had years of experience. *Trust me.*

Till Death Do Us Part

So listen, my children, and take it all in, the foolhardy fable of Bonnie and Jim.
'Twas late in the April of '72, 'fore the nightingale sang or the hoot-owls flew.
The sun cast rays through a sky dark-gray, and waiting in church was a bride in dismay.
The father of she who was to wed hurried up the aisle in obvious dread.
Speed it up, pastor, say the "I do's," The groom is unsure, and may bid his adieus
Hurry my daughter and kick it in gear, echo the vows and show no fear,
For tomorrow will begin your whole lifetime with him.

The years came and went, and richly were spent
There were promises broken and promises met,
We seldom erred far from the goals that we set
Some memories are golden, to each other beholden.
We loved and we learned, we laughed and we burned
Through his loan, our mortgage, a bra or two, and oft times even my stew.

The years have passed quickly, we've hardly been sickly.
Lucky stars are still shining, 'cause our pledge is still binding
We look back and shudder, "How young! we both mutter.
To many we're bold, but to some we're just old.
We built three houses, and still remain spouses.
I'm wise to him and his every trick, I don't need a Tom or a Harry or Dick
We're glued at the hip till we take that last trip.
We're husband and wife, despite any strife,
We'll sail into the sunset without guilt or regret
Till one of us dies, and the other one cries.
I'd mourn for two years and swipe numberless tears
Jim would be blue, with no one to talk to.
But soon he won't mind it as he learns the house will be quiet.
Though the end might be nigh, we'll keep eating blueberry pie.
We'll clip coupons galore, so we don't become poor,
Our dear daughter will weep, we'll leave her nothing to keep.
We'll go out with a roar, skipping through heaven's door,
And St. Peter will say, "What makes you okay?"
And we'll recount our life, and he'll say *"great wife"*
And Jim will say "Yes," she was the absolute best.
And I'll blush like a bride, but take St. Pete aside
And tell him the truth, and we'll wait in the booth
Till he consults with the Lord, Who is checking that board.
After much pondering, God will agree, and shoot us to Paradise where we'll ever be
And another mate I'll never seek, guess what? In heaven men can't speak.

*Section 5: Tidbits -
or why don't these have a unifying theme?*

When the Saints Come Marching In

In these difficult economic times, I was thinking how lucky I was that Joe was around to help me when we needed to sell our house. I knew about Joe—St. Joseph, the patron saint of carpenters to those of you that haven't met him or utilized his power. Being raised Catholic I had more than just a passing acquaintance with the saints. Even a few of my Protestant friends admitted they had asked for St. Joe's help. My good friend, who had just sold her house, told us about it one day during a game of Bridge.

"It's all because of my statue of St. Joseph," she said. "He did it! I know it was because of him!" She was ecstatic about getting a good offer.

"How?" I asked skeptically. "You prayed to him?"

"No, I buried him in my yard. If you do, you will sell your house." At that moment my partner bid three No Trump, and I forgot about statues for a while. Later in the week, as I passed the religious goods store, I thought, *Well, why not?* In I marched, past the rosaries, the holy water fonts, and the Sacred Heart pictures, straight over to the statues. By the time the clerk made her way over to where I was, I had already selected a six-inch statue of St. Joseph. Since I'm cheap by nature, I chose one without a box which made it a bargain at $5.99. After all, I was just going to bury him in the yard.

I drove home and in the tumultuousness of my daily life, I somehow misplaced the statue. But never fear, I prayed to St. Jude, the patron saint of lost causes and immediately found Joe under the front seat of my car, directly below my medal of St. Christopher, patron saint of travelers.

I worried that Joe might be angry about my callous treatment toward him and refuse to help me, so I handled him very gently, apologized profusely and fetched my shovel. I chose to put him under the day lilies because I thought he might like the cool shade of the leaves. I forgot about him again until a neighbor jogged my memory by inquiring about our "house selling status".

I told her about Joe resting peacefully in my back yard. "What!" she cried, "You can't bury him in the *back* yard. It has to be the front yard!" Lord, why aren't these important facts taught in school, or at the very least printed on the sides of cereal boxes? I raced to the garage, snatched my garden gloves, dug up Joe, and replanted him in the front yard near the peonies. I was sure that the beautiful, pink blossoms would remind him of heaven and bring out his best efforts on my behalf.

That night we went to dinner with my sister-in-law. I told her about the horrible faux pas I had made by putting Joe in the backyard.

"You planted him upside down, didn't you? You know it only works if he's upside down," she informed me. Good grief! Upside down? What else could I do wrong? "And he has to be facing your front door," she continued. Now I find that out! Shouldn't information this important be dispersed from the pulpit? Before the sun was up the next morning I donned garden gloves again and, bedecked only in my pink nightgown and fuzzy slippers, dug the poor guy up and replanted him upside down and facing the front door. I was worried that I had stretched his patience too thin.

He must not have been too miffed because two days later we got an offer on the house. Immediately upon hanging up the phone, I ran out, dug up Joe, washed him and gave him a place of honor on my window sill. Eventually he ended up in a crate going to the new house. I'm not sure what box he's in right now, but with the housing market this crazy, I'm willing to find him and loan him out. Just give me a day or two so I can pray to St. Anthony, patron saint of lost items.

Join the Club

Twenty years ago I started a Poker Club. Things went pretty well till one of our group members moved to another state. Darn, I missed her. Not just her friendship. It was because she was the only one of our members that outweighed me. We were the two amigos who helped ourselves to seconds, ate dessert when others claimed they were full, and had our hands in the candy bowl all afternoon.

Next to her, my thunder thighs looked downright svelte. Unfortunately, I could not enact a rule to allow only fatties to apply for her dual position as a member in good standing and also as the person that made me feel thin. The gal who took her place was a perky little thing wearing size-four slacks and a sleeveless blouse that flaunted arms that didn't jiggle. It was downright disgusting! Then, to add insult to injury, the majority ruled that we would no longer serve dessert. So, I quit.

Soon after, I heard about a new game called Bunko. It sounded easy and fun. I asked 11 of my nearest and dearest friends to come to my house for the inaugural event. I served a veritable smorgasbord. Each lady took her turn, of course, but nobody matched my pinnacle of fabulous food. Sadly, the majority of the group later decided it was too much work to prepare a buffet; we should only serve nutritious snacks. So, I quit.

I dutifully joined the Parent's Club at my daughter's school. They said to bring cookies to the next meeting. I was so excited. If we all brought cookies, I'd be in 7th heaven sampling everyone's favorite recipes. Boy, was I fooled. The goodies were for a bake sale for the following Sunday.

An acquaintance from A.A.U.W. called one day. Would I join the board? Flattery will get anyone anywhere with me, so, of course I humbly accepted. I told my husband, who stated that I was nuts to take on yet another project. I proudly told my mother who announced that they probably couldn't find anyone foolish enough to take the position. Undaunted, I attended my first meeting, and the best part was that the meetings were conducted over lunch.

After a nice welcome, it was suggested that I, as the new member, would be perfect to step into the role of the retiring member. I could head up the fundraiser for the scholarship fund. Yikes! I was expecting to help with something simple, maybe volunteer to call a few people for donations. Even with the promise of monthly lunches, I quit.

Let's see, what else have I quit? At Garden Club they always served petite canapés and finger food—who wants to eat miniatures? It gives new meaning to the word *rations*. For years I belonged to a Ladies' Golf Group. I only endured the golf for the lunch that followed. I tried Monday Afternoon Bowling, but no one wanted to go out to eat either before or after. I have my principles: food and fun must accompany each other. So, I quit.

There have been a whole slew of exercise programs I've dropped. Apparently, eating as a reward for exercising is not encouraged. There was Poker Club, which had great snacks, but got costly. Did I mention Gourmet Club? It had a lot of potential, but, good Lord, were we really expected to eat all that weird, unpronounceable cuisine?

I know gourmet is desirable to some people, but I don't know what I'm eating when all the descriptions have accents and umlauts and foreign words. And does the Surgeon General, or whoever says that certain things cause cancer, know what's in those choices?

There are a number of churches that no longer see me sitting in the pew. I mean, really, is the FDA inspecting those casseroles at the pot luck suppers? Weight Watchers? Quit. Curves? Quit. Alumni Board? Quit. Red Cross Board? Quit.

Rocky Road is Not Just an Ice Cream

Lest you think I quit everything, I will have you know I am a happy member of three Mah Jongg groups where we always eat lunch before we play. No danger of quitting one of those. And, my husband and I have been members of a Dinner Club for 35 years. I'm sure you can understand my loyalty from the inspirational name of the club. And we belong to a wonderful Couples' Golf Group in Arizona that always gathers afterward to imbibe in some liquid refreshments and solid nourishment.

So, feel free to ask me to join your club, group, association, board, organization, fraternity, league, guild, society, union, alliance, gang, sect, or faction, but please know that if you don't feed me, I will probably quit.

First Class? Any Class? No Class!

I would like to state once and for all that I do not want to become culturally aware, empowered, or improved. I want to read what I like, watch what pleases me and go wherever I want. Is that too much to ask out of life? At 60 plus years old am I really expected to elevate myself? Why can't I just be a lazy slug? No one has any expectations for you when you're a slug. You have one goal—don't get squashed. If all goes well, a slug never needs to cook, clean, iron, vacuum, or good grief, scrub the toilet.

Are you one of those people who are hooked on educational programs? I ask you, does The Learning Channel play reruns of *Diagnosis Murder*? No! Does the History Channel throw in a fairy tale ending now and then? Yeah, right! Talk radio? Please! Lectures on astronomy? Boring! And a violin concerto? The strings would be put to better use by strangling me to end my boredom.

I know you're sure I'll be enthralled and enriched by your recommendations, but you won't get me to fall for that fabrication more than once. I still have nightmares about going to the symphony and stifling my yawns till the much-awaited intermission (which I thought would never come), when I fled to my car and hurried home to my PJs and TiVo.

The Oprah Book Club book you insisted I read sits half-finished on my shelf, and I lost track of how long ago I lost the DVD on global warming you gave me. Nothing would appeal to me at the Guggenheim, I don't need to wear brand name clothes, and I'm sure that drinking water

Rocky Road is Not Just an Ice Cream

out of expensive crystal won't make it taste any better than it does in my complementary Kwik Trip thermal mug.

If you wish to phone me, please wait till after *Grey's Anatomy*, and don't ring my doorbell at 8 p.m. on Wednesday unless you plan to join me on the couch for *Modern Family*. To be truthful, I've been known to sneak in some PBS Theatre from time to time, but, just so we're clear, they have to be showing a murder mystery for my interest to be even vaguely piqued. I go to painstaking measures to avoid a book club, a bible study, or a political rally.

It's Motel 6 instead of the Ritz Carlton for me, and God forbid I'd shop at Gucci when TJ Maxx will do just fine. A big city represents outlet malls and a chance to go to a casino; I can skip the art galleries and museums. The only exception might be the Smithsonian Institute where one can actually see Archie Bunker's chair and Colombo's trench coat. I mean, how cool is that?

And speaking of restaurants (notice how my mind jumps to eating), my daughter is horrified that my favorite places are the comfortable and convenient chain restaurants that you can find all over the country. She has no appreciation for the words ALL YOU CAN EAT FOR $6.99.

Steinbeck, Hemingway, Tolstoy and Homer are all great names, but not if I have to read their tedious tomes. Give me a *Good Housekeeping* where I can find out really important things like how to clean a closet in one hour, turn turkey leftovers into 72 delicious dishes, and choose the best swimsuit for the *full* figure. And how could we all live fulfilling lives if we didn't have *People* to tell us what J Lo, Angelina, and the Kardashians wore on the red carpet?

When I set a table these days it's with disposable plates, plastic cups, and paper napkins. The goblets, bone china, and sterling silver service for 12 are history. It's not like the food ever makes it to the dining table most of the time, anyway; it just takes a little detour with me to my La-Z-Boy in front of the TV. That's the pinnacle of high cuisine at our house.

The only reason a self-professed couch potato such as myself would ever want to leave the comfort of my family room would be an enticing offer from my husband to go out for dinner. Any occasion that separates me from cooking is the very definition of sacrosanct in my world.

I'm capricious about my outings to the theater, too. Movies are a fun getaway, an escape from reality, and I don't much care that most of the movies premiering these days will probably erode my mind. My biggest dilemma is struggling with a very difficult decision each time I go to the theater—should I get the super-sized popcorn and soda with the free refills, or should I save my money for the big box of chocolate-covered malted milk balls? Should I make an attempt to be good while I'm *at* the movie so I can go for a pizza with the works *after* the movie? It's agonizing to make those kinds of decisions, so I save myself the grief and choose them all!

Go With the Flow

My husband and I live on the banks of the Mississippi in Minnesota. Each day I open the blinds to amazing things flowing past our windows—beautiful yachts northbound to Lake City and Stillwater, towboats guiding their loads south to New Orleans, seagulls diving for the debris churned by their powerful engines.

Without question, the most spectacular boats we have seen are the *Queens*. The *American Queen*, the *Mississippi Queen*, and the *Delta Queen*. They paddle along like floating hotels, trailing calliope music in their wake. We love to sit on our patio, sipping an ice-cold diet something (you can add your own libation here) and waving to the passengers. Unfortunately, some of those majestic ladies now sit in dry dock, their grace and elegance lost.

Besides various personal craft there have been some mighty strange water conveyances. It was more than a little disconcerting to look out and see a replica of the *Nina*. Or was it the *Pinta?* Or the *Santa Maria?* My husband says I should remember, as I was there for their original voyage. He is so funny...not!

Two summers ago a plane landed right in front of our patio. I was stunned, but it was clear the pilot knew what he was doing, so I cancelled the 911 call. He steered to a sandbar across from us and stayed for the weekend.

After we moved to the river, it didn't take long to notice that most non-motorized watercraft head south. Whether they're flotillas of people connected by inner tubes, lonely canoers, or pairs of kayakers, they all figured out one law of nature—it's easier to go with the flow.

Fishing boats of every size and color make their way in and out of the sloughs and quietly slip around our dock hoping the fish won't hear them and realize there's a human at the other end of the line. Having been suddenly and unceremoniously surprised by one of those fisherman, I now know to wear a robe in the mornings when I'm having my cup of tea on the patio.

I've also discovered the secret of how to keep overnight guests to a minimum—invite them to visit the same weekend as a bass fishing tournament. At the crack of dawn those boats whine by the guest bedroom windows at breakneck speed, seeking the best spot to capture the "big one."

Logs the size of small submarines often float by and just as often get caught on our dock, which never fails to drive my husband nuts. He's the one that has to push them away—I am much too petite and frail for such a demanding task. (Note to readers: if you knew me, you'd realize how much I stretch the truth.)

I'm not sure how to categorize parasailers. Crazy is usually the first word that comes to mind. Insane is next, most often followed by stark-raving mad. That might be a result of my fear of heights, falling from heights and landing after falling from heights, definitely in that order. They act like they're having the thrill of their lives, calling and waving as we landlubbers ooh and ahh, but, get real, they must be totally bonkers.

We loved the two shirtless Norwegians stuffed in a kayak, proudly flying their country's flag with music blaring and not a care in the world. They were probably crossing an item off their bucket list. I don't think floating down the Mississippi on something no bigger than a skateboard would be anywhere on *my* bucket list. Number one on my list would be to cruise around the world on a luxury liner—five stars, of course.

Some of the homemade rafts are fun to observe, although we mostly worry if they're sea worthy, especially when we notice that the skipper is hoisting a few. Several of these creative crafts have been powered by bicycles. I think the key to going 2,000 miles on a bicycle-powered boat is to have a *big* crew.

It was a few weeks ago when the latest adventurers floated by our house. They were two young men from England. Starting at the head waters of the Mississippi and making their way to the Gulf of Mexico, they stood—barefoot I might add—on *longboards* (they look like surfboards), using paddles to propel themselves.

The night we spotted them the air was sticky and steamy, and the drone of the mosquitos in their endless swarms only confirmed the rest of the night would be just as sultry. It was dusk and we had just finished dinner when we spotted them. I grabbed my camera and we ran out to see them. "Want a beer?" my husband shouted.

"Don't mind if we do," and within minutes they had their longboards tied to our dock. We added some supper to absorb their beers and enjoyed a few moments of "hands across the water." Within the hour they were on their way, equipped with doggie bags and naturally, a couple more beers.

The river has charmed me with its playfulness, frightened me with its ocean-like waves, excited me with its dark storms, calmed me with its mirror-like surface, and intrigued me by its beauty, power, and diversity. My husband says I should write a poem on its complexity, its muddy depths, and the sparkle of the moon on its surface. I wasn't listening; I was too busy daydreaming about a pirate ship mooring at my dock and a swashbuckling buccaneer, maybe Johnny Depp, running up to my door, knocking. Oh wait, did I say that out loud?

Needless To Say

When we started spending our winters in Arizona, we wanted a church to call home, so we visited many in the area. One weekend we went to a very old Spanish mission with a location that fit my criteria for all groups and organizations I contemplate joining—close to shopping and restaurants.

As the service began, we realized it was Confirmation Day. Two teenage girls walked up the aisle, one wearing a pretty confirmation dress with a white veil covering her bowed head. The other was, well, let's just say she was a *big* girl. Her outfit was also white; a white see-through blouse and skin-tight white jeans painted on her lower half. I won't even mention the high-heeled sandals. The sunshine coming in through the stained glass windows danced off the diamond studs that outlined the pockets on her rear end, drawing all eyes to her butt.

I turned to my husband and gave him my best *"don't you say a word"* look. My threat only delayed the inevitable. It all went downhill when the priest began Mass. He had an Eliza Doolittle cockney accent infused with testosterone. My wonderful husband, whom you already know I have to monitor 24/7, leaned over to me and in a stage whisper that carried over ten rows, said, "He must have really pissed off his boss in England to be banished to the Arizona desert." Needless to say we did not make St. Anne's our church community.

Speaking of stages and whispers, Jim and I took my 90-year-old mother to see one of my daughter's many dance recitals. We sat, along with other proud families, through dozens of ballet, tap and modern interpretation routines performed by oodles of budding ballerinas. A group of adorable six-year-olds were next on stage, dressed in their little pink tutus. One little darling was noticeably fluffier than the others.

My mother, who wore hearing aids, leaned over to me, and in a voice that could be heard in the next county said, "Why did her parents let her go up on stage when she's so fat?" Mortified, I shushed my mother, who again whispered in a voice even louder than before, "Oh, I'm just whispering; no one can hear me except you." Needless to say, that was the last performance I took her to.

When I was on a golf committee years ago, my friend Patty and I used to e-mail each other about the people we had to deal with each week during the meetings. Idiots, imbeciles, morons…well, I'll leave it to your imagination to speculate about the other uncomplimentary slurs we used. One day I wrote a particularly articulate correspondence to my friend, in which I used several interesting and familiar adjectives to relay my experience with a certain golf member. Instead of sending it to my friend Patty, however, I accidentally sent it to my *Aunt* Patty. Needless to say, I've learned to always double check the send line before I pop off an e-mail. I also request that the recipient destroy the evidence by printing it out and then eating it.

In the age before caller ID, my phone rang one day. "Hi, Bonnie, I haven't talked to you for ages." *I hate it when people don't identify themselves.* "Just wanted to see how things are going for you." *No clue yet about who this is.* "How are your folks?" *Lord, who is this?* "My mother still talks about how fun your wedding reception was."

Oh, this is Janice. "How is life in Tennessee?" I ask.

"I live in Colorado," she replies.

Oh, oh! "Who is this?" I finally ask. When she tells me, I realize I have guessed wrong. *Just my luck.* Needless to say, I now make everyone identify themselves immediately before the possibility of an awkward guessing game has a chance to manifest. I don't even trust caller ID. I'm pretty sure my only daughter is planning to put me in the nursing home soon because I keep asking her to identify herself after I pick up the receiver and she says, "Hi, Mom."

My best friend Mary and I like to take bus trips to the casino. It's important to this story that you know she's one month older than I. A few summers ago we were at a casino in Iowa, and after exhausting her pennies on the Wheel of Fortune machine, she came to watch me play Blackjack.

Being the polite, mid-western gal that she is, she offered to refill my soda and also to get soda for the elderly gentleman I was chatting with next to me. Shortly after she left to run her errand of mercy, he said, "Is she your daughter?" I nearly fell off my stool. He was embarrassed when I explained our relationship, but I told him he definitely made her day. Needless to say, I decided to always introduce Mary as my friend from then on.

Eons ago, when I was a young, flat-chested 8th grader, I spent all spring wishing my "fried eggs" would get bigger. The reason was Brick, the lifeguard from the previous year. He was going to notice me this summer and, if all went as planned, carry me off on his white steed. The other girls at the pool had boobs. I had to do something fast; summer was approaching.

Remembering my mother's words, "What God has forgotten, make up with cotton," I started to brainstorm. Kleenex? Tissue paper? Those would not withstand the water test. The plan I devised involved the pilfering of two handkerchiefs from my dad's drawer. I sewed them into my pink one-piece suit and bingo; I had created the world's first falsies. Well, what did I know back then?

I was positive I looked perfectly natural, never mind that I went from a size AA to a size B overnight. The next time I was at the pool I executed a perfect swan dive, knowing what a great impression I would make on the love of my life and future husband. As I came to the surface I checked to see if he was looking. He was. I gracefully hoisted myself up on the side of the pool, looking to see if he was *still* looking. He was. It was then I realized that one of my falsies was now on the outside of my swimsuit. Needless to say, I never swam again at that pool when Brick was on duty.

Just last summer I had a similar experience with malfunctioning undergarments. I went to rest in the restroom and while I was there I couldn't help but notice that there was something sticking out of my blouse. Upon further inspection, I realized it was the underwire from my bra. It had worked its way up and out. Laughing, I went back to the table to share the joke with my friends. One gal said she'd noticed it but didn't want to say anything cuz she thought it was a chemo port. Needless to say, I inspect my undergarments very carefully now.

My husband, the inveterate April Fool's jokester, told me my friend had called and said she was pregnant. I was so excited for her. I ran out to the car, drove over to her house and rushed in congratulating her. She seemed surprised, but thanked me anyway and invited me in for a coke. "So, what did your husband say when you told him you were pregnant?"

"I didn't tell him I was pregnant," she said.

"Oh, when did you find out?" I asked in confusion.

"Find out what?"

"That you were pregnant," I stated, as if to a mentally challenged person.

"I'm not pregnant," she answered, reciprocating the tone I used to speak to someone with limited mental faculties.

"Why did you tell Jim you were pregnant?" Notice I'm still not catching on here.

"Bonnie, how could I be pregnant? You came to visit me in the hospital last year when I had my hysterectomy." Needless to say, I no longer believe anything that comes out of my husband's mouth.

One last story. A fellow teacher at my school got fired. Terrible gossip that I am, I was telling the sordid tale to some gals at a luncheon. When we got up to leave, I turned to grab my purse, and can you guess who was in the booth right behind me, staring at me? Yup, you're right. It was "she who shall remain nameless." I was mortified. Needless to say, now I always crane my neck to make sure the person I'm gossiping about is not within ear shot. You thought I was going to say I learned my lesson and never gossiped about anyone again, didn't you?

Go Team, Go!

In the last decade or so, sports teams have been berated for their choice of mascots. Some teams that proudly displayed an American Indian logo were the Indians, the Red Raiders, the Fighting Sioux, the Redskins, and the Warriors to name just a few.

Despite the fact that many Native American tribes have spoken in favor of allowing the mascot names, edicts have been announced from on high in many states: change your name to something less offensive. I think I recall that the penalty originally was that offenders would be eaten by bloodthirsty cannibals, but then the ACLU (American Cannibal League Union) stepped in and put an end to that. Oh, all right, that's not true, but I'm certain there was going to be a hefty fine for noncompliance.

In an effort to help some of the teams conform, I have some new names to suggest. I can hear the announcer now: "Ladies and gentlemen, hopping out onto the field, determined to strike fear in the hearts of their opponents, let's give a big welcome to the Bouncing Bunnies." While the crowd cheers the home team, their opponents, the Falling Leaves, wave to their fans as they drift gracefully onto the field in their orange and green uniforms.

The Marshmallows, although puffed up for each middle school game by their coach, Graham Cracker, have a problem with their all-white uniforms. Their mothers picketed because it was so difficult to keep them clean and demanded the coach rename the team the Chocolate Bars.

Trying to be strong and fearless, the Spineless Wimps basketball team is not winning any of their games. Recent articles written about them suggest the rather unfortunate truth of them living up to their name. And who wouldn't quake in their boots if they had to face a team called the Cheesy Chipmunks? Attendees at their events say the smell alone helps them overpower their opponents.

I believe we have other issues to consider, also. Other wrongs to right. Other misnomers to correct. How can we vilify the schools and teams that use now-unaccepted vernaculars, but exonerate the schools that honor presidents who owned slaves? I say we need to change both school names *and* team names.

We really shouldn't have George Washington High, James Madison Middle, and Thomas Jefferson Elementary. At the very least, we need to bring to the forefront some of the more recent presidents. There could be the JFK Elementary School Piglets, or why not the Two Georges Bush Middle School Baked Beans? I'm sure someone would love to play for the Richard Nixon High School Deep Throats, and the kids at Jimmy Carter Elementary would be thrilled to be called the Peanuts.

There might be a few raised eyebrows when the Bill Clinton High School hockey team starts calling themselves the Charging Cigars, but the golf team at Dwight D. Eisenhower High can proudly tee off as the Allied Army. The Gerald Ford Middle School wrestling coach decided to change their name from the Klutzes to something less suggestive after so many wrestlers tripped over the mats.

The students at Theodore Roosevelt Technical College are trying to change their name, the Teddy Bears, because they are embarrassed that it sometimes shows up on their transcripts. Of course, FDR's namesake team, the Wheelies, are rolling right along.

A few schools have tried to rename their school after Barack Obama, but finding a team name has proven rather difficult—neither In the Reds nor the Trillion Dollar Debtors has appealed to the community,

Rocky Road is Not Just an Ice Cream

and one school board in Alaska that boasts a wonderful view of Russia from the science lab window called a halt to naming their school after Sarah Palin, agreeing that a team named the Riflemen probably did not promote the right image. Isn't it interesting how nonpartisan school names and team names can be when someone works on non-offensive alternatives?

Around The World in 80 Hours

Last week we traveled around the world. Not in 80 *days* suspended in a hot air balloon with Jules Verne and not in 80 *seconds* with Sheppard Smith on Fox News. No, we went around the world in 80 *hours*. We were in New York, Cairo, Paris, Italy, Florida, Hollywood, Camelot, Asia, and other exotic locales I can't even describe.

Okay, we weren't really in those glamorous spots, but we *were* in their representative casinos in Las Vegas where we were lucky enough to skip the inconvenience of exchanging our dollars for francs, marks, pesos, pounds or euros. Yes, my husband and I drove to—*gasp*—Sin City. We cruised from Arizona to Nevada along a long, dusty trail with an unending landscape of desert and mountains.

As majestic as that sounds, seven hours looking out the car window at the same sight is monotony overload. We've made this trip to Vegas for years, always crossing the Hoover Dam on our way to the City of Lights and being stopped for inspection by the border patrol agents.

Apparently a car full of white-haired snow birds from Minnesota isn't enough to raise suspicion from the serious-looking officers who peer into cars and assess terrorist tendencies, because we're always allowed to keep moving toward our gambling mecca. I'll bet there was some snickering as they waved us through, knowing we would be many smackeroos lighter when we returned.

A few years ago we embarked on a similar journey on the road to riches, and I vividly remember gazing up at the new, nearly-completed bridge precariously suspended miles above the highway we were on. I announced to my husband that when that behemoth was finished, we would be driving to Vegas via Canada. *Never* would I drive across that swinging, swaying, sliver of concrete above the canyon.

Oh, I suppose with enough martinis I could probably be persuaded to sail across on Evil Kneivel's motorcycle, but I'll save that story for a different occasion. So, this year the bridge was ready and waiting, and we had no choice but to cross it—well, except for that Canada detour which my husband nixed. As we approached, I gobbled my anti-anxiety pills, covered my head with my coat, slid onto the floor and hummed *Here I Come, Jesus.*

We made it safely across the bridge and into the Pacific Time Zone. Whew! With that hurdle behind me, I was anxious to get to the casinos and try my luck. After dinner, which is as essential to my day as breathing, I couldn't wait to park my behind in front of a slot machine and repeatedly punch the MAX button with practiced fingers. For a break, I like to slip over to the blackjack tables where I toss my chips on the familiar felt top and hope yet again that I will be ahead at the end of the hour.

Have you been to Vegas? Do you ever wonder how many traffic accidents happen because people (read, men) become mesmerized by the multicolored neon signs advertising topless go-go dancers? Before they know it, they've jumped the curb and their car is sinking into the dancing waters of the Bellagio. Oops! And where else but Las Vegas can you shop by gondola, see the city lights from the top of the Eiffel Tower, take a roller coaster ride around the skyline of Manhattan, cross a dragon-guarded moat, and sleep in a pyramid?

Jim and I have watched Vegas grow and grow and, oh boy, grow. I'm pretty sure some of that growth had to do with all of the money I left behind on previous trips. We've been going since 1977. In the old days we used to walk from casino to casino, enjoying candy from the M&M store, shopping for tacky t-shirts on the Strip, visiting the Liberace Museum, and searching for the cheapest blackjack tables. Now, with arthritis and dementia creeping upon me and extra fat unexplainably accumulating around my middle, I insist we just valet park and stay at one casino, the price of the blackjack tables be damned.

Of course, the money disappears into a dark abyss just as easily at any casino whether I'm playing Caribbean Stud, Three Card Poker, Spanish 21, Texas Hold'em, or Wheel of Fortune. And so begins my slow decline into pauperhood. With each passing hour I sink further in the hole, going from table to table, game to game and slot machine to slot machine trying to find the one that will open its hidden caches.

I'm always waiting for the big bonanza—the payoff that will guarantee my picture (with a huge grin on my face, of course) ending up on the lobby wall holding the six-million dollar check I win. Visions of magnificent mansions, stretch limos, shopping sprees, overflowing closets, and my very own chef and butler dance in my head.

I *know* I'll hit the jackpot with the very next shuffle. Well, maybe this next pull…okay, perhaps if I walk over to the other side of the casino… better yet, leave this establishment, where they apparently have no clue that I'm supposed to become a millionaire and walk to the next casino—a 30 minute trot if I'm lucky. And yes, of course, I'll share my winnings with the federal government and my daughter and my husband, who deserves a reward for living with for 40 years, but the rest will be mine, *mine*, MINE!

I guess all that daydreaming about impending riches distracted me from finding the right machine, or maybe Lady Luck was occupied with someone else. The trip home was unusually subdued this year. I didn't chatter on about future fortunes, I didn't once mention how I was going to buy myself some diamond earrings, and I definitely refrained from mentioning the promise I made to have a huge gala with my winnings.

I sat sadly in my seat, slumped against the door, not even noticing that we had crossed over that dreaded bridge again. I was in a funk until my husband told me he had won as much as I had lost. What? Well, hot diggity-dog! We were even-steven! That was perfect. No harm, no foul. They say that what happens in Vegas stays in Vegas. Well, my money is one of those things that *stays* in Vegas.

It Was a Dark and Stormy Night

"Have you read so-and-so's latest novel?" asked one of my friends.

"No," I said, dreading the tiresome and predictable next comment.

"Oh, it's so good. I'll lend you my copy. You'll love it."

Except I *won't* love it. Maybe if I was marooned on a desert island and it happened to wash ashore, I might find a redeeming quality or two in it. It's probably even on Oprah's book list. I have to admit that I'm just not that interested. I don't want to read books that will enlighten me. You know—books that are read by every book club this side of the Mississippi. Books revered like a Pulitzer Prize winner as they're passed from one woman to another. Familiar titles like *The Hunger Games, Sarah's Key,* and *The Help.* Books that drift from house to house until finally coming to rest seductively on a library shelf under a sign that says "*New York Times Best Seller Ten Weeks in a Row.*" Nope, that's not my genre. I like to read murder mysteries.

"Uh-huh," she said, looking at me like I'm missing an important chromosome, "I'm sure *those* books are fine, too."

Fine? What can be better than breathlessly reading a who-done-it? I love the classic corpus delicti with characters both dastardly and daring. There's the murder victim—well not a victim yet because the author wants us to glimpse the *future* victim by painting him or her as a dim, dismal, deceptive, double-dealing dolt so when he or she dies, we're not upset.

Occasionally the author turns the tables and starts with a murder that happened *before* page one. In that case it's usually someone sweet

Rocky Road is Not Just an Ice Cream

and dearly missed by his or her family and we start right out hating the villain, whomever that might be. I always root for the handsome police officer or the dashing private detective or sometimes it's a Miss Marple character. I always become so involved with her that I feel like we're sisters in Sleuthdom, partners in pursuit and companions in crime solving. *We* will be triumphant over evil, *we* will live to solve another case in the sequel.

As a reader of non-fiction my daughter doesn't see the value of my reading preferences. She doesn't understand the draw of homicide as entertainment. "How does it enhance you?" she asks. "What do you learn from your hours invested in the book?" She has clearly never been beckoned by the likes of Agatha Christie, Mary Higgins Clark, James Patterson, Tami Hoag, or Vince Flynn.

"But, Mother, you know what the ending will be. The good guys win, the bad guys die or go to prison, and the heroine gets the hunk in the end." Precisely! The predictability of a murder mystery is one of the many things that make it so satisfying! The best part is that I *know* it will end well. Sometimes, if I can't stand the suspense any more, I cheat and look at the last page, just to see if the swarthy, seductive stranger who appeared in the middle of Chapter Three is still around at the end of the story. I don't actually read the ending, of course, but I *do* want to know if that tall, muscular cowboy who appears just in time to rescue the female detective is going to be the lover, the killer, or both.

I want you to know that I have the same plebian tastes in *all* aspects of my life. I watch *Storage Wars*, I hum to elevator music, and I drink boxed wine. So if you want me to join you in your haughty and ostentatious activities you'll have to let me bring popcorn to the opera, paste a bare-chested picture of Pierce Brosnan on the cover of your recommended tome, and convince PBS to have commercials so I can have a potty break. So please don't ask me to join your book club. Unless, of course, you're serving Oreos.

Sticks and Stones May Break Your Bones, but Words Can Hurt Forever

My mother was always telling me I needed to stand up straight, hold my head up high, suck in my tummy, and cross my legs at the ankles. It was her mantra for years. She wanted me to be Doris Day, Grace Kelly and Loretta Young—graceful, beautiful and praised. Of course, I definitely didn't jump to the conclusion that she saw potential in me to achieve those things, oh no. I can recognize disappointment and embarrassment a mile away.

To my mother, perfection was just this side of Heaven's gate. I guess I was off climbing trees with the boys or skinning my knee falling off my bicycle or, horror of horrors, exploring the muddy sand piles of the new house being built down the street. In other words I was absent the day God passed out perkiness, poise, and good posture.

In third grade I did what all kids do, I looked at my face long and hard in the mirror. Was I as pretty as the popular girls in the class? How did my hair compare? Of course, I found my features lacking. I would let my hair hang forward, trying to cover my face, never drawing attention to myself. One day during class, one of the popular boys whispered, "Hey, Pug Face, can I borrow a pencil?"

Did I let him borrow my pencil? Of course! Do you think I'm nuts? He was a *popular* boy, and he asked *me* for my pencil. I was honored by his attention. Thankfully, I finally learned that it wasn't worth enduring demeaning remarks to be part of the "in crowd," but what did I know in third grade?

After we were married, I noticed that my husband never sang in church. When questioned, he said, "Oh, my high school teacher told me to just mouth the words." The worst thing about this revelation was that he did not take umbrage at her insensitivity. Instead, he did as he was told. He quit singing forever.

Once in a while my daughter would say that her professor/boss/girlfriend/boyfriend/bus driver didn't like her. Later, she told me that the teacher gave her an A, the boss promoted her, the girlfriend asked her to be the maid-of-honor at her wedding, the boyfriend asked her to the prom and the bus driver...well, who knows?

When she was in fifth grade, a preteen taking ballet lessons, she worried that she would never be graceful on stage. She was frustrated because the ballet teacher didn't work with her during class. By not hearing the positive, she assumed the negative. One night she came out to the car smiling. The instructor had pointed out to the class how well she had done her plié-de-cocovin-a-l'orange or whatever the French words are for "leaping through the air gracefully and landing without breaking a leg."

The teacher told her after class how happy she was to have my daughter as a student because she did everything so well and didn't need the teacher's constant attention. Did she sense Ann's mood? I don't know. What I do know is that Ann doubled her efforts, took every class she could, was accepted into the performing dance company the next year, and went on to dance in Colorado, Chicago, New York and Russia.

My best friend and I went to our 20th class reunion a while back. No, you don't need to know how many years ago that was. During the obligatory pre-dinner phase of the festivities, the committee played a CD of every photo ever taken during our high school years. It was a horrifying hour that chronicled our progress from frightened freshmen to sophisticated seniors. You know, geeky to gorgeous in four short years.

As I sat, mortified, hoping that we would have an electrical outage, a really neat thing happened—the MC, scrolling through the pictures, stopped at one that featured my girlfriend and said, "There's Mary; she was such a cutie." My girlfriend had never dated much in high school; she was the smart one, the talented one, the one on the yearbook committee, the math team, and the debate club, and at our 20th reunion, had not yet married. The words the MC spoke made her feel wonderful, special, and most of all, he made her feel like a cutie. It was a truly remarkable thing he did for her, and he never even knew it.

A word of cheer, a word of encouragement, a word of sympathy, a *word*, any word, spoken with sincerity and kindness can accomplish so much. And words uttered without thought to someone's pain, their self image, their feelings, can live forever in their hearts. I could claim that I'm perfect; that I'm always complimentary to people. That I'm the sweetest mom this side of the Rio Grande and the kind of wife that husbands worldwide seek, but you know for sure that isn't true. I usually think of what I *should* have said about two seconds after it has tumbled out of my mouth. Sticks and stones might break your bones, but a kind word never hurt anybody.

Baubles and Bangles and Bling, Oh My!

The first two weeks of February in Tucson are magical. You can follow the yellow brick road (better known as Irvington Road) to get to the Emerald City (better known as the Gem Show). Once granted entrance to the tents, the glitter and glow of jewelry and beads from the far corners of the world assault your eyes like prisms of light reflecting off a crystal.

Newcomers to the Tucson Gem and Mineral Show are immediately overwhelmed by the sheer magnitude of tables laden with jewels of every shape and size. If you are a seasoned traveler along the road to riches, you draw in a deep breath and start your journey. As you pass booth after booth, you find yourself in Morocco, Russia, Indonesia, Holland, India, Mexico, Spain, and countries that you haven't heard of since that fifth grade geography test you barely passed.

I am a seasoned veteran Gem Show goer, but I once felt like Dorothy trying to navigate the yellow brick road. I've long ago passed the point of being overwhelmed by the clutter and have honed my skills to a science. It's blatantly obvious to me that the booths are manned by the Munchkins that think I'm a scarecrow with no brain. I personify the heartless tin man when I gaze at trinkets that would strip my pocketbook of all its contents and I run like the cowardly lion when I get close to the glass-encased 14-karat gold selections.

Sometimes I bring newbies to the tents. Wide-eyed, they follow me like Toto, afraid if they leave my side they'll be swallowed up in the poppy fields and never find their way to the wizard's door. Yes, it can be a treacherous road to follow; fraught with flying monkeys in the guise of people peddling their wares and sometimes a wicked witch waiting at the gate ready to yank fraudulent credentials if you try to sneak in.

After all, only true believers can be allowed inside to peruse the endless heaps of jewels and precious stones. Booths are chock-full of every adornment known to womankind, with some special items for men, too. If you're not a lover of all things sparkly, you do not belong in the City of Emeralds…and diamonds and pearls and rubies and sapphires.

Case in point: one year I insisted that my husband attend the show with me to see why I was enamored with turquoise and coral and jasper and tanzanite; watches and rings and beads to adorn every part of my body. I wanted him to see the attraction, the pull, the lure of endless bargains for fingers and necks and ears and wrists, but instead of appreciating my charmed world, he decided to have a heart attack right there at the Gem Show. The nerve of that man! In retrosepct it might have been a little callous of me to tell the ambulance attendants I'd follow them in a couple hours—after the tents closed.

It can be dangerous in other ways, too. You could easily trip on the trillions of taped-down electrical wires, you could be blistered by the millions of watts of overhead lighting, and getting lost along the thousands of avenues lined with loot is always a high probability. A GPS could help perhaps, but what would be the fun of that? It's much better to click your ruby slippers and wish yourself to your desired destination, and sure as there are hot air balloons in the sky, you'll eventually reach home with the fruits of your labors stuffed in boxes and bags.

Wishing to avoid the danger of giving my husband a second heart attack when he saw the credit card statement, I told him that it wasn't my fault that a tornado swept through the tent and deposited all the excess baubles and bangles and bling from the Gem Show into my Kansas—I mean *canvas*—bag. Oh, in case you were wondering, my husband still lives and the Gem Show continues on. Look for me, I'll be the one wearing the blue and white gingham dress and carrying a basket with a little black dog in it.

Writer's Blockage

Okay, what to write for my next column? Sometimes I mull over possible themes for days. Many times at the end of the day I have nothing on my laptop. I used to think my mind was like a steel trap, but unfortunately I think it rusted shut several years ago.

I have a well-planned writing routine. Monday I put idea to paper, or in this case, computer. Tuesday I rewrite, grateful that no one saw Monday's draft, which to most would look like it was written by someone who'd had a few too many margaritas. On Wednesday I call my girlfriend and force her to listen to my quote unquote "witty remarks peppered with my sassy sense of humor."

I then do another rewrite and print it for my husband with a note asking for his comments. Later I find my untouched essay. When I ask for some verbal feedback, he says, "It was fine." *Fine?* I want more than fine, but I know that's all I'll get from Mr. Helpful. Last step…read it out loud so I'm prepared for the true test—my newspaper readers.

Meanwhile, back to this week's problem. What to write? I went to the San Diego Zoo last year. It was fun, but it wasn't funny. I could certainly write pages comparing my life to life in a zoo. Saw the elephants—need to make an appointment for a facial. Enjoyed the lions—need to make an appointment for a waxing. Monkeys were silly—need to make an appointment with a psychologist. Observed two-toed sloth—need to make an appointment for a pedicure. Where else can I go with all that information?

Rocky Road is Not Just an Ice Cream

I've toyed with the idea of writing a diet book. After all, who has been on more diets that I? I'd call it the *Play with Your Food Diet*. The requirements would be that you reconfigure your food into some other shape before eating. Shoelaces out of French style green beans, ear muffs out of orange halves, poker chips out of Ritz Crackers. All that creative activity would take time, therefore keeping you from eating too much and, if all goes well, it would pretty much completely ruin your appetite, which would bring on the same results of not eating—weight loss! I think I'll table the diet book for now.

The other day I thought maybe I could write an entire narrative on cleaning out closets. However, to accomplish that goal I would need to buy my daughter a china hutch, some shelves, and well, a house, so that I can just slide my treasures (better known as junk) over to my daughter, thereby absolving me of any decision making responsibilities in disposal and distribution. So, there it is, I've exhausted that topic. What more is there to say?

Someone mentioned that they wrote an ode to a sugar maple tree. I thought, wow, cool, what could I write an ode to? Ode to a snake? Ode to a cantaloupe? Ode to *Gray's Anatomy*? Ode to curling irons? I thought on that for all of ten minutes and nothing inspired me to even write the first line. Another column thwarted before it ever got to paper.

Late last night I had an idea. I could write an essay on games. Games I enjoy playing but never win, even when I'm the score keeper. Like Trivial Pursuit. I think I got *one* answer correct back in 1987. Forget Scrabble, I kant speell wurth a darne. Monopoly is monotonous. Clue is fun, but I keep getting distracted with the cute little game pieces and never have a "clue" who done it. I played Bridge for 30 years but hated every cotton-pickin' minute of it. I mean, really, can't we just say how many spades and hearts we have, instead of that *über* secret Charles Goren language?

I'm pretty good at Crazy Eights. It's a game that's simple enough for me to play, talk and eat at the same time. I'm into Mah Jongg these days, but mostly because we meet for lunch first. How can you beat any activity that begins or ends with food?

Okay, here we are at D-day. Obviously my muse is out to lunch—I think I'll join her. Of course, what I really need is some Metamucil for my mind to take care of that *blockage*.

Acknowledgments

I would like to first and most importantly thank my daughter, Ann Willemssen, for her enthusiastic encouragement, her excellent suggestions, and her utmost patience when I kept screwing up the computer.

After you read this book you will know why I heartily thank my husband, Jim, for being the brunt of most of my stories. He has been such a good sport and has put up with a lot of teasing.

I could not have succeeded without the help of my best friend, Mary Kroner, who listened to my first, second, third, and fourth drafts of every column. So many of the clever ideas were hers. I call her Saint Mary.

I also depended on my friend/editor extraordinaire, Pat Poehling, for unfailingly finding all my grammar, spelling, and punctuation errors. Who knew slew and slough were two different words and for Pete's sake, does the world really need all those commas?

A special thank you to Debbie Kramer for reading and laughing at my stories.

Diana Hammell, my friend who works for *The Caledonia Argus*, asked me to write a piece for her newspaper about living on the

Mississippi River and it turned out to be my very first humorous column. Without her this book would not exist. Because my columns were not online, I forwarded them to my friends and relatives who gave me super feedback. I wanted to keep writing to entertain them, so thank you for your support. Also, it was always nice to open my email and find a note from an appreciative reader. Having strangers take the time to write and tell you how much they enjoyed your work is very gratifying.

My Green Valley writer's forum witnessed the birth of my first humorous story. It was written about five years ago and their response (applause) was so encouraging that I kept writing a short story for each week's meeting. Many of those stories were turned into columns years later. I especially want to thank Denise Roessle from the Society of Southwest Authors for asking me numerous times to read my work at the annual SSA Author's Showcase. It was always an honor to be asked and a thrill to be laughed at. Also, with Denise's encouragement, I began a working relationship with Dan Shearer at *The Green Valley Sun and Times*.

I was encouraged to compile this book by so many friends and relatives. To that purpose, I found a wonderful professional editor at RedWillowDesignServices@gmail.com, Rob O'Byrne. His creativity and immediate understanding of my voice allowed me to relax and let him do his thing. He had to deal with my obvious lack of computer skills, but undaunted, he soldiered on. Last but not least, I'd like to thank Debbie O'Byrne for her cover art.

Rocky Road is Not Just an Ice Cream

No one can tell me that writing is a lonely job. It is not. It is a joy to write and share my stories with all of you.

Please write and tell me your thoughts on my book. BONNIEWILLEMSSEN@GMAIL.COM or visit my website at www.bonniewillemssen.wordpress.com.

Made in the USA
Charleston, SC
11 November 2012